JOB SEARCH AND CHECKLISTS

101 Proven Time-Saving Checklists to Organize and Plan Your Career Search

By Arlene S. Hirsch

JIST Works
Works
America's Career Publisher

Job Search and Career Checklists

101 Proven Time-Saving Checklists to Organize and Plan Your Career Search

© 2005 by Arlene S. Hirsch

Published by JIST Works, an imprint of JIST Publishing, Inc.
8902 Otis Avenue
Indianapolis, IN 46216-1033

Phone: 1-800-648-JIST   Fax: 1-800-JIST-FAX
E-mail: info@jist.com   Web site: www.jist.com

About career materials published by JIST: Our materials encourage people to be self-directed and to take control of their destinies. We work hard to provide excellent content, solid advice, and techniques that get results. If you have questions about this book or other JIST products, call 1-800-648-JIST or visit www.jist.com.

Quantity discounts are available for JIST products. Please call 1-800-648-JIST or visit www.jist.com for a free catalog and more information.

Visit www.jist.com for information on JIST, free job search information, book excerpts, and ordering information on our many products. For free information on 14,000 job titles, visit www.careeroink.com.

Also by Arlene S. Hirsch: *How to Be Happy at Work*

Acquisitions Editor: Randy Haubner
Development Editor: Stephanie Koutek
Cover Designer: designLab, Seattle
Interior Designer: Aleata Howard
Interior Layout: Carolyn J. Newland
Proofreaders: Linda Seifert, Jeanne Clark
Indexer: Henthorne House

Printed in Canada

08 07 06 05 04   9 8 7 6 5 4 3 2 1

Library of Congress Cataloging-in-Publication Data
Hirsch, Arlene S., 1951-
    Job search and career checklists : 101 proven time-saving checklists to
    organize and plan your career search / y Arlene S. Hirsch.
         p. cm.
    Rev. ed. of: VGM's careers checklists. c1991.
    Includes index.
    ISBN 1-59357-118-6 (alk. paper)
  1. Vocational guidance--Handbooks, manuals, etc. 2. Job hunting--Handbooks,
    manuals, etc. 3. Career development--Handbooks, manuals, etc. I. Title.
  HF5381.H517 2005
  650.14--dc22   2004025534

We have been careful to provide accurate information throughout this book, but it is possible that errors and omissions have been introduced. Please consider this in making any career plans or other important decisions. Trust your own judgment above all else and in all things.

Trademarks: All brand names and product names used in this book are trade names, service marks, trademarks, or registered trademarks of their respective owners.

ISBN 1-59357-118-6

About This Book

The job market is a place of staggering confusion and complexity that requires savvy career decision-making and job hunting skills. This book has been created in checklist format to help you identify and develop the skills that you need to be successful in the job market.

This book is written for anyone who is involved in making a career choice, career change, or job change. The checklists in this book can be used either as stand-alone exercises or as a comprehensive career guidance manual. You can work through the checklists on a step-by-step basis or go directly to those checklists that address your specific needs and concerns.

The book is divided into five sections. The first section is designed to help you chart a career path. It uses a variety of self-assessment exercises along with job market exploration tools to help you understand where fit you best in the world of work.

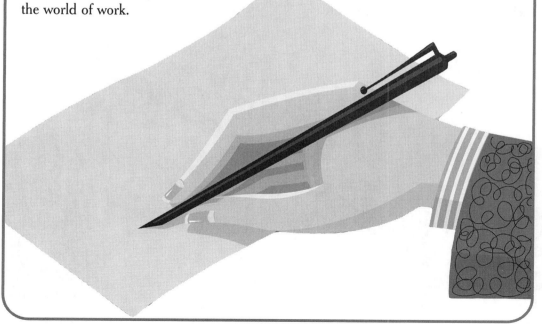

The second section is designed to help you write an effective resume and cover letter. You can use these checklists to determine which format to use, learn how to effectively present information about accomplishments and experience, and discover other valuable resume tips. This section also provides extensive information about how to write great cover letters that not only get read, but make employers sit up and take notice.

The third section covers the essential components of a job search strategy: networking, informational interviewing, direct marketing campaigns, Internet research, and other valuable tools to create and implement a successful job search campaign.

In the fourth section, you will find lots of information about the interviewing process: how to prepare for an interview, anticipate both typical and difficult questions, develop rapport, manage illegal queries, and negotiate salary and other forms of compensation.

The final section addresses a number of critical career decisions: how and when to leave a job, change careers, go back to school, or start a new business. Taken together, these five sections should enable you to decide upon and implement effective changes in your work life.

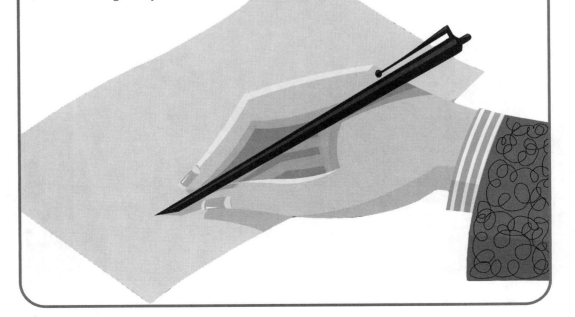

Dedication

To Ruby—

first father, first love.

Acknowledgments

I would like to thank Randy Haubner, Stephanie Koutek, and Acacia Martinez, my colleagues at JIST, for their guidance and support. Without them, this book would not have been possible.

Table of Contents

SECTION 3: A-Job-Hunting We Will Go 85

Key Skills in Career Planning and Decision-Making

The goal of Section 1 is to help you figure out who you are and where you fit in the world of work. In this section, you will find a number of checklists to help you with the process of self-assessment and job market research.

1. The Ten Commandments of Career Satisfaction and Success

There is a wisdom of the head, and . . . a wisdom of the heart.

Charles Dickens

1. Honor your talents, interests, and values.

2. Choose a career that matters to you.

3. Build more competence every day.

4. Learn from your mistakes.

5. Seek out mentors whom you respect and admire.

6. Be an individual performer and a team player.

7. Strive for visibility.

8. Accept responsibility for your successes and your failures.

9. Keep things in balance and perspective.

10. Cultivate a supportive network of people for the good times and the bad.

© JIST WORKS

2. Seven Rules for a More Successful Career

The future belongs to those who believe in the beauty of their dreams.

Eleanor Roosevelt

Rule 1: Motivation is the key to success.

The key to understanding personal motivation is in knowing what energizes you—what kinds of activities, people, places, and situations are personally stimulating and fulfilling—and then capitalizing on those motivations.

Rule 2: Success takes hard work.

Success takes preparation and hard work. Thomas Edison once remarked, "A genius is a talented person who does his homework." Bill Gates was a computer geek before he was catapulted into the limelight. Michael Jordan was a hardworking and determined high-school and college athlete before he became one of the greatest athletes of all time. These men are rich, but they devoted themselves to their work, have been willing to work hard, and haven't been daunted by failure.

Rule 3: Learn from your mistakes.

Success depends on learning from mistakes and overcoming challenges.

It's not enough to be ambitious. The world is filled with ambition, and the path to success is littered with discarded dreams and disillusioned people who never achieved the recognition or success they felt they deserved.

Rule 4: Follow your dreams.

Missions are the values or dreams that drive super-achievers to pursue excellence. Clinical psychologist Charles Garfield researched super-achievers in business to learn what made them different. In his book *Peak Performers* (Avon, 1991), he reveals that these executives achieve consistently impressive and satisfying results without burning out because "they went and pursued their dreams." In every peak performer, Dr. Garfield found a desire to excel at something the person truly cared about.

Rule 5: Honor your talents.

When Harvard University psychologist Howard Gardner conducted his landmark research on multiple intelligences, he opened the door to a fuller understanding of human potential. In contrast to society's traditional emphasis on verbal and analytical abilities as the pinnacle of intelligence, Dr. Gardner put forth a more expanded vision that includes linguistic, musical, spatial, kinesthetic, emotional, interpersonal, and intrapersonal intelligences. Understanding yourself as a multifaceted individual with many talents and possibilities enables you to expand your vision of your own career potential.

Rule 6: Manage yourself.

There's no direct correlation between success and mental health. You don't have to be a nice person to be successful. You *can* win the rat race and still be a rat. But if you manage yourself well, you can win the rat race without *turning into* a rat. This involves developing a good working relationship with your thoughts, feelings, and actions.

Rule 7: Take calculated risks.

Most of us were raised with rules and know the consequences of disobeying them. But if those rules have taught you that it's dangerous to take risks, you are limiting your rewards. When building a career in the competitive work world, you must be willing to take risks to reap the rewards you seek. Successful risk-taking involves knowing your risk tolerance. What many otherwise ambitious careerists fail to realize is that *not taking a risk is also a risk*. There's a risk involved in *not trying*, and along with the risk of failing, there's the risk of regret.

3. Knowing What You Do Best

What lies behind us and what lies before us are tiny matters compared to what lies within us.

Ralph Waldo Emerson

To determine your best career choices, you must be able to identify and build on your skills and abilities. In the following checklist, I ask you to give more thought to those dimensions of yourself. Rate yourself Excellent, Good, or Fair on each skill and then choose your top ten skills in each area.

SKILLS WORKING WITH PEOPLE	
Skill	**Rating (Excellent, Good, Fair)**
Acting	
Advising	
Advocacy	
Arbitration	
Clarifying	
Client/customer relations	
Coaching	
Collaborating	
Communicating	
Conflict management	
Consulting	
Counseling	
Creating synergies	
Debating	
Decision-making	

(continued)

(continued)

SKILLS WORKING WITH PEOPLE	
Skill	**Rating (Excellent, Good, Fair)**
Delegating	
Demonstrating	
Developing people	
Diplomacy/tact	
Directing	
Effecting change	
Entertaining	
Facilitating	
Helping others	
Hosting	
Influencing	
Initiating	
Instructing	
Interrogating	
Interviewing	
Leadership	
Listening	
Litigation	
Managing people	
Mediation	
Mentoring	
Monitoring	
Motivating	
Negotiation	
Nurturing	
Performing	

SKILLS WORKING WITH PEOPLE	
Skill	**Rating (Excellent, Good, Fair)**
Placating	
Policing	
Promoting	
Public speaking	
Recruiting	
Representing	
Sales	
Socializing	
Supervising	
Teaching	
Team-building	
Training	

Summary of Top Ten People Skills

1. _____

2. _____

3. _____

4. _____

5. _____

6. _____

7. _____

8. _____

9. _____

10. _____

SKILLS WORKING WITH DATA AND THINGS

Skill	Rating (Excellent, Good, Fair)
Accounting	
Analyzing	
Appraising	
Assessing	
Auditing	
Bookkeeping	
Budgeting	
Calculating	
Cataloguing	
Charting	
Classifying	
Compiling data	
Computer programming	
Conceptualizing	
Creating	
Designing	
Drafting	
Drawing	
Driving	
Editing	
Evaluating	
Experimenting	
Financial planning	
Fund-raising	
Forecasting	
Formulating policy	
Hypothesizing	
Interpreting	

SKILLS WORKING WITH DATA AND THINGS

Skill	Rating (Excellent, Good, Fair)
Inventing	
Investing	
Machine operation	
Mechanical aptitude	
Planning	
Policy analysis	
Policy development	
Problem analysis	
Problem-solving	
Program design	
Program development	
Project design	
Project development	
Project management	
Reading blueprints	
Reducing costs	
Regulating	
Reorganizing	
Researching	
Reviewing	
Scheduling	
Spatial relations	
Surveying	
System analysis	
System design	
Testing	
Troubleshooting	
Typing	
Using tools	

Summary of Top Ten Skills with Data and Things

1. _____

2. _____

3. _____

4. _____

5. _____

6. _____

7. _____

8. _____

9. _____

10. _____

4. How Motivated Are Your Skills?

Nothing great was ever achieved without enthusiasm.

Ralph Waldo Emerson

During the course of your career, you may have developed lots of skills and abilities that you prefer *not* to continue to use. When evaluating future career choices and options, you want to be sure to capitalize on the use of what we call *motivated skills*. Just as the term implies, motivated skills are the ones that you find energizing and enjoyable.

Review the exercise from Checklist 3 to determine which skills you really enjoy using and want to continue to use and develop. List your motivated skills below. If you would like to continue to enhance these skills, you can set learning goals for yourself that will enable you to become increasingly proficient at things you enjoy.

Motivated Skills Working with People

1. _____

2. _____

3. _____

4. _____

5. _____

6. _____

7. _____

8. _____

9. _____

10. _____

Motivated Skills Working with Data and Things

1. _____

2. _____

3. _____

4. _____

5. _____

6. _____

7. _____

8. _____

9. _____

10. _____

5. What Do You Like to Do? The Power of Interests

Do what you love, the money will follow.

Marsha Sinetar

Psychologist John Holland developed a well-known classification system that you can use to organize your thinking about your interests. He believed that most people can categorize their interests according to six types: Realistic, Investigative, Artistic, Social, Enterprising, and Conventional.

A review of these categories may help you define your strongest areas of vocational interest. Keep in mind that most jobs and occupations combine aspects of several interest categories instead of falling under the exclusive domain of any one category.

- ✔ **Realistic**: Individuals with realistic interests prefer activities that involve working with tools, machinery, or animals. They often enjoy working with their hands and being outdoors. Typical realistic jobs include engineers, machinists, and farmers.

- ✔ **Investigative**: Investigative people are usually analytical, methodical, precise, and curious. They enjoy solving complex mathematical problems, scientific inquiry, and research. Typical investigative careers include biologists, mathematicians, research scientists, and physicians.

- ✔ **Artistic**: Artistic individuals are often creative, non-conforming, original, and introspective. They tend to like flexible, unstructured environments that value innovation and creativity. Typical occupations include artists, writers, designers, and musicians.

- ✔ **Social**: People with social interests enjoy helping and teaching others. They are often social workers, counselors, teachers, and bartenders.

- ✔ **Enterprising**: Enterprising individuals are often drawn to the business world. They enjoy influencing, persuading, and leading others for the purpose of economic or organizational gain. Salespeople, attorneys, and managers are often enterprising types.

- ✔ **Conventional**: People with conventional interests enjoy working with data and paper. They are often drawn to jobs or professions with high levels of administrative activities, such as accountants, secretaries, and administrators.

6. A Second Look at Your Interests

The courage to imagine the otherwise is our greatest resource,
adding color and suspense to all our life.

Daniel Boorstin

Because your likes and dislikes are such an important dimension of career success and satisfaction, I'm including a checklist to help you identify your strongest areas of interest.

List ten activities that you particularly enjoy (for example, going to movies, reading books, baking a cake).

1. _____

2. _____

3. _____

4. _____

5. _____

6. _____

7. _____

8. _____

9. _____

10. _____

List ten occupations that interest you. (Don't worry about whether you have the ability to be successful in the occupations.)

1. _____

2. _____

3. _____

4. _____

5. _____

6. _____

7. _____

8. _____

9. _____

10. _____

List ten subjects or topics that you would like to learn more about.

1. _____

2. _____

3. _____

4. _____

5. _____

6. _____

7. _____

8. _____

9. _____

10. _____

When you have completed these lists, you may want to take a trip to the library or the bookstore or go online to find out more about how those interests can become a integral part of your career.

7. 25 Work-Related Values

The life which is unexamined is not worth living.

Plato

Recognizing your values is an important part of the self-assessment process. Review the following work-related values and rate them 1-5 (with 1 being most important and 5 being least important). Then summarize your most important values at the bottom of the page.

_____ money	_____ power
_____ job security	_____ flexibility
_____ autonomy	_____ work–life balance
_____ affiliation with people you like	_____ growth
_____ safe working conditions	_____ variety
_____ location	_____ leadership
_____ benefits	_____ challenge
_____ interesting work	_____ meaning
_____ making a contribution	_____ technical competence
_____ innovation and creativity	_____ prestigious organization
_____ opportunities for advancement	_____ resources
_____ professional development	_____ other_____
_____ recognition	_____ other_____
_____ challenge	_____ other_____

Values Summary: _____

_____

_____

8. Personality Type

The shoe that fits one person pinches another;
there is no recipe for living that suits all cases.

Carl Jung

One of the most popular personality profiles is the Myers-Briggs Type Inventory, which uses four dimensions of personality to help individuals determine their specific personality type.

Extraversion	Introversion
Extraversion (E) means that you are energized by the outer world of people rather than the inner world of ideas.	Introversion (I) means that you are energized by and relate more easily to the world of ideas.

Sensing	iNtuition
Sensing (S) means that you prefer to work with concrete, practical facts and are oriented toward the present tense.	Intuition (N) means that you prefer to work with possibilities and relationships rather than facts.

Thinking	Feeling
Thinking (T) means that you base your judgments on impersonal analysis and logic.	Feeling (F) means that you base your judgments more on personal values and feelings than objective analysis.

Judging	Perceiving
Judging (J) means that you prefer a planned, orderly, structured way of life and are often results-oriented.	Perceiving (P) means that you prefer a flexible, spontaneous way of life and may be more process-oriented.

9. Working Conditions

It's no measure of health to be well adjusted to a profoundly sick society.

Krishnamarti

Although you may not get everything you want, it is important to determine your work priorities and negotiate for the things that are more important to you.

Put a check mark next to the conditions that you consider non-negotiable (in other words, your must-haves).

_____ short commute	_____ on-the-job training
_____ casual work environment	_____ fast pace
_____ flexible schedule	_____ holiday pay
_____ private office	_____ room for advancement
_____ job security	_____ privacy
_____ reasonable hours	_____ state-of-the-art technology
_____ on-site day care facility	_____ tuition reimbursement
_____ employee parking	_____ family leave policy
_____ company car	_____ good working conditions
_____ performance bonuses	_____ professional working environment
_____ nice offices	_____ other _____
_____ liberal vacation policy	_____ other _____
_____ sick leave	_____ other _____
_____ insurance benefits	

10. Some Things You Need to Know About Career Testing

If you think you can do a thing or think you can't do a thing, you're right.

Henry Ford

For those readers who are interested in a more objective form of self-assessment, it often makes sense to invest in vocational testing. Here are some guidelines to keep in mind:

1. **There is no perfect test that is right for everyone.** The goal of vocational testing is to help you understand yourself better in order to make better career decisions. When choosing the right test for you, you need to find a comfortable format as well as the right content.

2. **Tests make more sense when interpreted by experts.** Experts are familiar with what the results mean and can help you figure out how to make the best career decisions based on that information. If you aren't familiar with the range of tests available, seek out the services of a qualified career counselor to help you make that determination and interpret the test results.

3. **There is no perfect answer.** A test will not provide you with the "perfect answer" to your career choice questions. It can only provide guidelines to help you discover the best answers for yourself. Although it's understandable to want a test to tell you who are and what you should do, the real value of tests is exploratory. A good test can provide new insights and ideas.

4. **If one is good, then two (or three or four) are better.** Take a variety of tests in order to get a more comprehensive picture of your skills, interests, preferences, and personality style. When you take a whole series of tests, you are in a better position to identify overlapping and complementary themes.

5. **Tests are designed to facilitate self-knowledge, not replace it.** No test results should ever be treated as gospel if they don't seem accurate to you. They can't provide easy answers to serve as a substitute for genuine soul-searching. Trust your intuition. Always listen to your heart.

6. **You are more complicated than your test results.** While test results can seem uncannily accurate, they are always, at best, approximations of who you are. Rather than viewing them as a complete picture of yourself, use them as a basis for further exploration.

11. Choosing the Right Test

Know then thyself.

Alexander Pope

When it comes to vocational testing, you can find a variety of self-assessment resources that can help you get in touch with your "vocational self."

✔ **Personality tests** include personality-type or temperament indicators, such as the Myers-Briggs Type Indicator (MBTI), Enneagram, the Sixteen Personality Factor Questionnaire (16PF), and the Keirsey Temperament Sorter. They provide information on how you prefer to communicate, gather information, and make decisions and how your style compares with others'.

✔ **Interest inventories** offer suggestions for careers based on your personal interests. They include the Strong Interest Inventory, the Self-Directed Search, and the Campbell Interest and Skill Survey, among many others.

✔ **Skills tests** help define your skills and abilities. You'll often find them bundled with interest inventories. Others exist as stand-alone tests for specific job areas. Unfortunately, the skills tests appear to be the weak link in the testing arsenal, which means you may have to use alternative approaches to skill assessment in order to determine what you're really good at. (See Checklist 10 for an alternative to skills testing.)

✔ **Values inventories** allow you to examine what motivates you and what is important to you. A few possibilities include the Study of Values, Super's Work Values Inventory, the Career Values Card Sort, and the MAPP test.

12. Brainstorming for Job Ideas

This time, like all times, is a very good one,
if we but know what to do with it.

Ralph Waldo Emerson

Self-assessment is an important part of the career choice process, but it is also essential to marry that assessment to your understanding of a dynamically changing job market. The following list is designed to increase your knowledge of job possibilities. Read through the list and circle job titles that interest you. If you are not familiar with a particular job title (but would like to learn more about it), put a question mark next to that particular title as a reminder to do some research.

A

Accountant

Accounting clerk

Activities therapist

Actor

Actuary

Acupuncturist

Addictions counselor

Administrative assistant

Adult education instructor

Advertising executive

Aerobics instructor

Agent

Air traffic controller

Airline pilot

Analyst

Animal trainer

Animator

Anthropologist

Antique dealer

Appraiser

Archaeologist

Architect

Archivist

Art dealer

Art director

Art teacher

Art therapist

Artist

Artist's representative

Astrologer

Astronomer

Athlete

Athletic coach

Athletic director

Athletic trainer

Attorney

Auctioneer

Audiologist

Author

Auto dealer
Automotive body repairer
Automotive mechanic
Aviation engineer
Aviation mechanic

B

Bail bonding agent
Baker
Banker
Barber
Bartender
Beautician
Belly dancer
Biochemist
Biogeneticist
Biological weapons expert
Biologist
Biology teacher
Biomedical engineer
Bodyguard
Book binder
Book editor
Bookkeeper
Botanist
Brand manager
Bricklayer
Broadcast journalist
Broadcast technician
Building contractor
Building inspector
Building manager
Bus driver
Business home economist
Buyer

C

Cake decorator
Candy maker
Captain
Cardiologist
Career coach
Career counselor
Carpenter
Cartographer
Cartoonist
Cashier
Caterer
Chauffeur
Chef
Chemical engineer
Chemist
Chemistry teacher
Child care worker
Child psychologist
Child welfare worker
Chiropractor
Chocolatier
Choreographer
Cinematographer
City manager
Civil engineer
Civil engineering technician
Claims adjuster
Climatologist
Clinical psychologist
Clown
College admissions officer
Columnist
Comedian

Comedy writer

Commercial artist

Commodities trader

Communications consultant

Community activist

Community educator

Community relations director

Competitive intelligence analyst

Compliance officer

Composer

Comptroller

Computer equipment repairer

Computer game tester

Computer graphics artist

Computer operator

Computer security specialist

Computer systems analyst

Conductor

Conservationist

Conservator

Construction worker

Consultant

Convention/conference planner

Cook

Copy writer

Coroner

Corrections officer

Cosmetologist

Costume designer

Court reporter

Credit analyst

Credit officer

Criminologist

Cross-cultural trainer

Croupier

Cruise director

Curator

Customer service representative

Cytotechnologist

D

Dance choreographer

Dance teacher

Dance therapist

Dancer

Data processing operator

Data processing supervisor

Day care director

Dean

Dental assistant

Dental hygienist

Dentist

Design engineer

Designer

Detective

Development officer

Diamond cutter

Diesel mechanic

Dietitian

Diplomat

Director

Disc jockey (Announcer)

Dispatcher

Distance education instructor

Diver

Diving instructor

Dog groomer
Dog trainer
Dog walker
Dollmaker
Drafter
Drama coach
Dramateur
Dressmaker
Driver

E

Ecologist
Economist
Editor
Educational administrator (Principal, Superintendent)
Educational psychologist
EEG technologist
EKG technician
Electrical/electronic engineer
Electrician
Elementary school teacher
Emergency medical technician
Employee assistance counselor
Employee benefits specialist
Engineering technician
Engraver
Entertainer
Environmental attorney
Environmental educator
Environmental engineer
Environmentalist
Ergonomics engineer

Estimator
Evangelist
Examiner
Excavator
Executive assistant
Executive coach
Executive recruiter
Executive secretary
Exercise physiologist
Exporter

F

Facilities engineer
Family life educator
Family therapist
Farm manager
Farm operator
Fashion designer
Fashion illustrator
Financial analyst
Financial director
Financial planner
Firefighter
Fisher
Fitness instructor
Flight attendant
Floral designer
Florist
Food scientist
Food service supervisor
Food service worker
Foreign service officer
Forensic accountant

Forensic pathologist
Forensic psychologist
Forest ranger
Forester
Freelance writer
Fundraiser
Furniture designer
Furrier

G

Game designer
Gamekeeper
Gardener
Gemologist
Genealogist
General contractor
General manager
Genetic counselor
Geneticist
Geodetic surveyor
Geographer
Geologist
Geophysicist
Geriatric nurse
Geriatric social worker
Gerontologist
Glass blower
Glazier
Government chief executive
Graphic artist
Graphic designer
Groundskeeper
Guidance counselor
Gynecologist

H

Health care administrator
Health care worker
Health educator
Health physicist
Historian
History teacher
Home inspector
Horse trainer
Horticultural therapist
Horticultural worker
Hospice worker
Hospital administrator
Host
Hotel clerk
Hotel manager
Housekeeper
Housekeeping supervisor
Human resources director
Human resources representative
Hypnotist

I–J

Illustrator
Image consultant
Immigration attorney
Importer
Industrial engineer
Industrial hygienist
Information specialist
Information systems consultant
Inspector
Installer
Instructional designer

Instructor
Insurance broker
Interior designer
International meeting planner
Interpreter
Interviewer
Inventor
Investigator
Investment banker
Ironworker

Janitor
Jeweler
Job counselor
Journalist
Judge

L

Labor attorney
Labor relations specialist
Laboratory technician
Landscape architect
Landscape gardener
Law librarian
Lawyer
Legal assistant
Legislative aide
Legislative analyst
Legislator
Librarian
Linguist
Literary agent
Loan officer

Lobbyist
Lyricist

M

Machinist
Magician
Maintenance engineer
Make-up artist
Management consultant
Manager
Manufacturer's representative
Map editor
Marine biologist
Marine geologist
Marketing assistant
Marketing communications director
Marketing research analyst
Massage therapist
Materials scientist
Mathematician
Mechanical engineer
Media relations specialist
Mediator
Medical assistant
Medical examiner
Medical illustrator
Medical photographer
Medical records clerk
Medical social worker
Medical technologist
Mental health worker
Metallurgist
Meteorologist

Microbiologist
Military (enlisted)
Military officer
Minister
Model
Mortgage broker
Mortician
Motivational speaker
Motorcycle mechanic
Music therapist
Musical instrument repairer
Musician
Musicologist
Mycologist

N

Nanny
Naprapath
Naturalist
Navigator
Neurologist
Neuropsychologist
Newspaper columnist
Newspaper editor
Newspaper publisher
Newspaper reporter
Newswriter
Nuclear engineer
Numerical control (NC) machine-tool
   operator
Nurse
Nurse-anesthetist
Nurse-consultant

Nurse educator
Nurse-midwife
Nurse's aide
Nursing home administrator
Nutritionist

O

Obstetrician
Occupational health and safety
   inspector
Occupational therapist
Oceanographer
Office manager
Operations manager
Ophthalmologist
Optician
Optometrist
Oral surgeon
Organizational psychologist
Osteopath
Otolaryngologist
Outplacement consultant
Outreach worker

P

Painter
Paleontologist
Paralegal (Legal assistant)
Park ranger
Parole officer
Party planner
Pathologist
Patient representative

Pawnbroker
Payroll clerk
Pediatric nurse
Pediatrician
Penologist
Personal injury attorney
Personal shopper
Pharmacist
Pharmacy technician
Photogrammetrist
Photographer
Photojournalist
Physical therapist
Physician
Physician assistant
Physicist
Physiologist
Piano tuner
Pipe fitter
Plumber
Podiatrist
Poet
Police officer
Political scientist
Politician
Preschool teacher
Priest
Producer
Professor
Program analyst
Program director
Proofreader
Property manager

Prosthetist
Psychiatrist
Psychoanalyst
Psychologist
Psychometrist
Public affairs specialist
Public relations representative
Publicist
Publisher
Purchasing agent

Q–R

Quality control specialist
Quality engineer

Rabbi
Radio announcer
Radio producer
Radiologic (X-ray) technician
Radiologist
Reader
Real estate developer
Realtor
Receptionist
Recording engineer
Recreational director
Recruiter
Referee
Registrar
Rehabilitation therapist
Reporter
Research assistant
Researcher
Reservations agent

Respiratory therapist

Restaurant manager

Restoration architect

Restorer

Retail manager

Roboticist

Roofer

S

Safety inspector

Sales agent

Sales person

School nurse

School psychologist

Science teacher

Science writer

Scientist

Scout

Screenwriter

Seamstress

Securities trader

Security officer

Sheet-metal worker

Seismologist

Set designer

Shop steward

Singer

Ski instructor

Skip tracer

Social worker

Sociologist

Software developer

Sound mixer

Special events director

Speech pathologist

Speechwriter

Sports agent

Sportscaster

Statistician

Stockbroker

Store detective

Stunt person

Surveyor

Systems engineer

T

Tattoo artist

Tax analyst

Tax attorney

Teacher

Technical writer

Theater manager

Tool and die maker

Tour guide

Tour operator

Toy designer

Trainer

Translator

Travel agent

Travel clerk

Trucker

Trust officer

Typist

U–V

Ultrasound technician

Underwriter

Upholsterer

Urban planner
Urologist
Utility worker

Veterinarian
Veterinary technician

W–Z

Waiter
Webmaster

Wedding consultant
Welder
Wildlife conservationist
Woodworker
Writer

Youth counselor

Zookeeper
Zoologist

Occupations Summary

Occupations that interest me:

1. _____

2. _____

3. _____

4. _____

Occupations that I want to research:

1. _____

2. _____

3. _____

4. _____

13. Researching the Job Market Through Informational Interviewing

If you're not confused, you're not paying attention.

Tom Peters

With so many changes in the job market, it's no wonder that so many people find researching a career confusing and overwhelming. The key is to find ways to link your self-assessment information to potential career choices and then structure a plan to learn more about the fields and industries that interest you. Informational interviewing, a targeted form of networking, is an essential part of that process.

Here's how it works:

1. Use the Occupations Summary in the previous checklist to identify the fields and occupations that you want to explore.

2. Ask people that you know (relatives, acquaintances, friends, colleagues, past employers) to introduce you to people who work in your areas of interest.

3. Use the *Encyclopedia of Associations* (available at many libraries) and other resource materials to help you identify professional/trade associations in your target area. If there is a local chapter, plan to attend a meeting to meet new people and learn more about the field.

4. Should you decide to join a professional group, ask if they have a membership directory (which you can use to conduct further informational interviews) as well as a job bank (which will come in handy when you're ready to do your job search).

5. When you have identified the people that you want to meet (either through your personal networking strategy or by using the directory), contact them by e-mail or phone to schedule a convenient time to talk.

6. During your initial conversation, make sure that you briefly explain who you are, why you are contacting them, and what you hope to gain from the conversation. Make sure that you are cordial but assertive.

7. Before the interviews, do your homework. Read trade journals, track down Web sites, and gather whatever information you need in order to present yourself as a knowledgeable interviewee. Remember that your goal is not to find a job, it is to find out if this is the right career path or company for you.

8. At the conclusion of the interview, ask your contact if they can recommend other people or resources that you can use to learn more about your areas of interest.

9. Always follow up your meetings with a thank-you letter. If someone was particularly helpful, make sure that you tell them how much you appreciate their interest and concern. Also, make sure that you periodically apprise them of your progress. They will surely appreciate your consideration.

10. After you have made a decision (whether it's for or against a particular choice), reconnect with your network of people to let them know how you are progressing and what you would like to happen next.

14. Questions to Ask in Informational Interviews

Life is rather like a tin of sardines—we're all of us looking for the key.
Alan Bennett

Come to informational interviews prepared with a list of questions and, if necessary, take notes during the interview to make sure that you remember the answers to your questions. The following questions will (hopefully) get your thinking started in the right direction:

1. What is your job title and occupational role?

2. How did you choose this field? Profession?

3. What kind of training do you need to do your job?

4. What skills and experience do you need to work in this field?

5. What is your educational background?

6. Do you think that your education prepared you well to do this kind of work?

7. Do you have an area of specialization?

8. Are there other areas of specialization that I might want to consider?

9. What does a typical career path look like in this field?

10. Is the field growing?

11. What are the most difficult challenges that you face in your work? Career?

12. How competitive is this field? Are jobs plentiful or scarce?

13. How do you typically spend your day? Week?

14. Do you work under a lot of stress?

15. How many hours per week do you normally work? Is it common to take work home?

16. Do you have to deal with a lot of crises and emergencies?

17. Where does your job/position fit within the larger organization?

18. Do people recognize and appreciate the work you do?

19. What do you like most about this work?

20. What do you like least about this work?

21. What advice can you give me?

22. Is there a professional group that you like and belong to?

23. Can you recommend other people for me to talk to?

24. If I want to go into this field, what do you recommend that I do first?

25. Is there anything that you wish you had done differently in your career?

26. What is a typical starting salary?

27. Would you mind reviewing my resume and making comments?

28. What is the best way to find a job in your field?

15. Informational Interviewing Worksheet

Name of contact person: _____

Position/job title: _____

Company/organization: _____

Address: _____

Telephone: _____

Fax: _____

E-mail: _____

Web site: _____

Method of contact (letter, e-mail, telephone): _____

Date of first contact: _____

Purpose of interview: _____

Results: _____

_____

Follow-up: _____

Date of follow-up: _____

Purpose of follow-up: _____

Results of follow-up: _____

_____

Name of referral: _____

Contact information for referral: _____

Comments/notes regarding the referral: _____

_____

_____

16. Tapping into the Internet for Occupational Information

Getting information off the Internet is like taking a drink from a fire hydrant.

Mitchell Kapor

The growth of the Internet has proven to be a real bonanza for people who are looking for occupational information. The sites listed below offer free access to

- ✔ occupational outlooks and trends
- ✔ requirements for specific jobs
- ✔ earning potential for specific jobs
- ✔ working conditions for specific jobs

America's Career InfoNet

www.acinet.org

Provides data from a variety of federal and state sources, including information about typical wages and employment trends across occupations and industries. You can check education, knowledge, skills, and abilities against requirements for most occupations and learn about state-by-state labor market conditions.

Career Browser

www.collegeboard.com/apps/careers/index

Comprehensive site offering descriptions on hundreds of occupations relevant for all workers regardless of experience level, including working conditions, current employment, training, job outlook, earnings, and related professions.

Career Voyages

www.careervoyages.gov

Sponsored by the Department of Labor and the Department of Education, this career exploration tool offers resources and information, including the hottest occupations with the fastest growth rate and most job openings.

Guides for Specific Careers

www.jobstar.org/tools/career/spec-car.cfm

Explores more than 40 career fields. Typical resources include the type of training and/or education, earnings potential, work environment, and personal accounts from individuals working in the specific fields.

O*NET (Occupational Information Network)

www.onetcenter.org

Comprehensive database of information on skills, abilities, knowledge, work activities, and interests associated with more than 1100 occupations. The O*NET currently contains information developed by job analysts using the O*NET skill-based structure, which has replaced the Dictionary of Occupational Titles.

Occupational Profiles

www.vault.com

Profiles for more than 50 occupations include an overview, skills required, career path, salary, and general work environment information. Additional features include "A Day in the Life" profiles of professionals in top careers and industry overviews. Some areas of the site require the purchase of a subscription.

Resumes and Cover Letters

Resumes and cover letters are essential job search tools. In this section, you will find out how to create the most effective resumes and cover letters for your situation.

17. Building Blocks of a Good (Chronological) Resume

Many a small thing has been made large by the right kind of advertising.

Mark Twain

A resume is a self-marketing tool that is designed to showcase your skills, achievements, and experience. Its primary purpose is to help you obtain the interest of potential employers. To write an effective resume, you must learn the fine art of selling yourself.

The following guidelines will point you in the right direction:

1. The very first thing that a reader should see on your resume is your contact information. This includes your name, address, telephone number, e-mail address, and, if appropriate, cell phone and fax numbers.

2. If your goal is to create clarity and focus, you should opt for the use of a professional objective. It is especially helpful if it is not clear from your previous experience what kind of position you are looking for.

3. A profile or summary is a concise snapshot or overview that can be used to summarize your qualifications and experience.

4. List your work experience in reverse chronological order: name and location (city, state) of employer, job title, dates of employment, and major responsibilities and accomplishments.

5. Next is your educational experience, including name of institution(s), degree(s) received (or dates of attendance), major or primary course of study, and relevant extracurricular activities.

6. Then, include licenses, certifications, and additional training, including the name of the institution and the name and date of the license or certification. For coursework, include the name of the course, dates attended, and granting institution.

7. In addition, list honors and awards such as grants, scholarships, fellowships, dean's list, or other forms of special recognition. Be sure to include the name of the honor, the granting institution, the date granted, and (if appropriate) a description of the activity.

8. The community and/or professional activities section can include any volunteer experiences with non-profit organizations, religious institutions, and professional trade associations. Again, include the name of the institution, the dates you participated, and the nature of your involvement (for example, board member or committee chair).

9. List any relevant technical skills you have. The section on technical skills usually includes hardware, software, and applications expertise.

18. Your Resume in Action: Verb(alizing) Your Accomplishments

Action may not always bring happiness,
but there is no happiness without action.

Benjamin Disraeli

Resumes should always be action-oriented. The following list of action verbs is designed to help you better identify and articulate your accomplishments.

Action Words

Achieved	Balanced	Constructed	Drafted
Acquired	Benchmarked	Consulted	Edited
Adapted	Briefed	Contributed	Educated
Administered	Broadened	Coordinated	Engineered
Advised	Built	Counseled	Established
Advocated	Chaired	Crafted	Evaluated
Allocated	Checked	Created	Exceeded
Analyzed	Clarified	Decreased	Executed
Anticipated	Collaborated	Defined	Expanded
Appraised	Combined	Delivered	Expedited
Arranged	Communicated	Demonstrated	Facilitated
Assembled	Completed	Designed	Financed
Assessed	Compiled	Determined	Foresaw
Assisted	Composed	Developed	Formalized
Attended	Computed	Diagnosed	Formed
Audited	Conceived	Directed	Formulated
Augmented	Concluded	Discovered	Fostered
Authored	Conducted	Documented	Founded

Generated	Linked	Promoted	Set up
Governed	Maintained	Proposed	Sold
Hired	Managed	Provided	Spearheaded
Identified	Marketed	Publicized	Sponsored
Implemented	Mediated	Published	Staffed
Improved	Mentored	Purchased	Started
Increased	Moderated	Pursued	Structured
Influenced	Monitored	Recruited	Supervised
Initiated	Motivated	Reengineered	Surpassed
Installed	Negotiated	Represented	Surveyed
Instituted	Operated	Researched	Taught
Integrated	Organized	Reshaped	Tested
Interacted	Originated	Resolved	Trained
Interpreted	Oversaw	Restructured	Transformed
Interviewed	Patented	Reviewed	Updated
Introduced	Performed	Revised	Upgraded
Invented	Pioneered	Rewrote	Utilized
Investigated	Planned	Scheduled	Wrote
Launched	Prepared	Secured	
Led	Produced	Selected	
Leveraged	Programmed	Served	

Words to Avoid Like the Proverbial Plague

Abused	Embezzled	Manhandled	Stole
Accused	Fired	Massacred	Squandered
Bullied	Immolated	Misappropriated	Threatened
Burned	Indicted	Robbed	Victimized
Destroyed	Maimed	Shot	Violated

19. One Size Does Not Fit All: Choosing the Best Resume Format

The more alternatives, the more difficult the choice.

Abbé D'Allanival

Your experience and target objective are the best determinants of what resume format makes the most sense for you.

Chronological resumes are, by far, the most recognized and widely used format to present your qualifications. The hallmark of this resume format is that it presents your work history in reverse chronological order. This enables employers to scan your resume quickly to determine whether you have the right qualifications and experience for the job. If your background is a less-than-perfect match, you may need to consider alternative styles that present your qualifications differently.

Functional resumes are also sometimes referred to as "skills-based resumes" because they place the emphasis on what you can do rather than on what you have done in the past. This format enables you to de-emphasize work history and focus on your skill set. It also enables you to group relevant skill sets together for greater emphasis. But the format comes with a *caveat emptor*: some employers are suspicious of this format because they suspect that you may be trying to hide something from them.

Combined resumes include elements of both the chronological and functional formats. They may include a shorter chronology of job descriptions preceded by a short Skills and Accomplishments section or a Summary of Qualifications that includes major skills and accomplishments.

Targeted resumes are created with specific jobs (or job objectives) in mind. If you keep your resume in a file on your computer, it should be relatively easy to tailor each resume to the specific position that you are applying for.

Scannable resumes are much like traditional resumes—minus the formatting. They have all of the same headings and information but don't include boldface, underlining, bullets, italics, font changes, and other design characteristics so that they can be scanned electronically. Many employers search resumes for keywords, so you need to review any known employment information (job title, responsibilities, and so on) and include that language in the body of your resume. Scannable resumes are also good to use when you are applying for a job online because they don't lose their formatting when you send them via e-mail.

Curriculum vitae (CVs) are created specifically for academic jobs. The CV is usually much longer than a traditional resume because it includes a complete list of grants, research projects, publications, and presentations.

Portfolios are visual resumes that are often used by people in creative or artistic fields to showcase their work. They may be presented in oversized leather or plastic briefcases and contain pictures, photographs, articles, illustrations, and other creative products, and they are often accompanied by a traditional resume.

20. The Brave New World of Electronic Resumes

To err is human, but to really foul things up requires a computer.

Farmers' Almanac, 1978

The key to creating a scannable resume is to make sure that it is readable by both employers and computers. Because these resumes are usually scanned into a company's human resources database, some special rules apply.

1. Print your resume on scannable high-quality laser-resolution paper.

2. Do not use colored paper or ink.

3. Send an original document rather than a photocopy.

4. Your name should appear on the first line of your resume with your address, phone number, e-mail address, and fax number beneath your name.

5. Your resume should include text only. Eliminate all bullets, underlining, graphics, italics, and boldface.

6. Keep the formatting simple. Use standard paragraphs, traditional fonts (Arial, Times, or Helvetica), and 10- to 14-point font size.

7. Make sure that you number the pages and put your name at the top of every page.

8. Don't use headers or footers.

9. Distinguish section headings by using capital letters.

10. Use an outline format (rather than bullet points) for your job responsibilities and accomplishments.

11. Use job-specific keywords. Industry terms, jargon, buzzwords, and hard skills will also pass the computer scan test for relevance. You can also include job titles, departments, key functions, technical skills, degrees, and other relevant information.

12. To adapt your current resume into a scanner-friendly resume, eliminate all the formatting and add a keywords section at the bottom of your resume.

21. From Good to Great: Making Your Resume Stand Out

Strive for excellence, not perfection.
H. Jackson Brown, Jr., *O Magazine,* December 2003

1. You never get a second chance to make a first impression.

   Research shows that only one interview is granted for every 200 resumes received by the average employer. You have only 10 to 20 seconds to persuade a prospective employer to read further, which means that you need to pass the first-glance test by making the first few lines really count.

2. Start with a goal in mind.

   If your goal is to persuade the hiring manager or recruiter to call you for an interview, you must entice them with your abilities and experience. If you are responding to an ad or have some idea of what kinds of skills and experience make an ideal candidate, you can shape your resume to include that information at the beginning of your resume. Although customizing your resume in this way obviously takes extra time, it is also a great way to position yourself to stand out from the competition. Only you can decide if that is time well spent.

3. A professional objective can lend clarity to an otherwise ambiguous document.

   The way to demonstrate your clarity of direction is to have the first major topic of your resume be your objective. Of course, it goes without saying that your job objective needs to match up well with the job that you are applying for. If you are making a career change, the job objective becomes even more important because it is not obvious from your work history what you are looking to do next.

4. If you elect to use a profile or summary, it replaces the professional objective.

   A profile or summary consists of several concise statements that focus the reader's attention on your most important qualities, experiences, and accomplishments. A well-written summary enables you to efficiently highlight the qualifications that make you an exceptional candidate.

5. To write a great summary, you must ask yourself what makes a person an ideal candidate for the position.

   Shape your summary in a way that demonstrates how perfectly you are suited to the position.

6. Focus on results.

   The body of your resume is composed largely of your skills and accomplishments. Whenever possible, quantify your skills and accomplishments to reflect stellar performance. It's not enough to recite your duties and responsibilities. Employers want to know what you achieved above and beyond the basics.

7. To power up your accomplishments, you may want to create a separate section called "Skills and Accomplishments" or "Summary of Accomplishments" that separates your specific results from everyday activities and responsibilities.

   Should you choose this style, remember to list your skills and accomplishments in order of importance to the employer. In other words, keep in mind what kind of results the reader is most likely to value and appreciate and list those achievements first.

22. Putting Your Education to Work

What sculpture is to a block of marble, education is to a human soul.

Joseph Addison

Which aspects of your education you choose to emphasize depends a lot on your individual circumstances. These general guidelines will help you get the credit you deserve for the education that you have achieved.

1. If you are a new graduate with limited work experience, you will want to put the education section of your resume near the top of the first page. Ramp it up by including information about scholarships, GPA, internships, work-study programs, related coursework, and extracurricular activities.

2. If you graduated more than five years ago, your job objective will determine whether you put your education before or after your work experience. If you are working in a field that is related to your degree or major, your work experience should receive the greater emphasis (and therefore go first). If you are working in an unrelated area and want to get back to your initial game plan, put your education before your work experience.

3. If you are a career changer with a new degree, put your education before your work experience. This structure will illustrate your commitment to and enthusiasm for your new career choice.

4. If you received your degree from a very prestigious university whose name impresses people, place the education section before your work experience to establish instant credibility.

5. If you are an academic, always put your education first.

23. Sample Profiles

*Experience is that marvelous thing that enables you to recognize
a mistake when you make it again.*

Franklin P. Jones

Resume profiles are concise snapshots or overviews of your qualifications and experience. They often include

✔ A short phrase describing your profession

followed by

✔ A statement of broad or specialized expertise

followed by

✔ two or three additional statements

related to

✔ Breadth, depth, or unique combination of skills

✔ Range of environments in which you have experience

✔ Special or well-documented accomplishment

and

✔ One or more professional or appropriate personal characteristics

Examples:

✔ Highly motivated human resources generalist with six years of experience in recruitment, training, employee relations, and benefits administration. Excellent organization, communication, and platform skills. Knowledgeable in consumer products and retail industries.

✔ Financial management executive with nearly ten years of experience in banking and international trade, finance, investments, and economic policy. Innovative skilled negotiator with strong management, sales, and marketing background. Expertise in mergers and acquisitions, commercial lending, and policy analysis.

✔ Resourceful and innovative health care administrator with program development, project management, and marketing experience. Extensive background in public health, critical care, and emergency medical services. Proven ability to develop quality programs and services with limited budgets and resources.

✔ Broadcast journalist with extensive reporting and announcing experience. Areas of expertise include news, politics, sports, and community affairs. Strong personality and screen presence. Ability to communicate at all levels of an organization.

✔ Over ten years of public relations experience in agency and corporate environments. Strong creative and account management skills. Expertise in media relations, event planning, and promotions.

✔ Sensitive and empathic psychiatric social worker with extensive experience in individual and group psychotherapy. Experience with personality disorders, mood and anxiety disorders, substance abuse, and other psychological disorders. Skilled clinician, supervisor, and administrator. MSW.

✔ Liberal arts graduate with strong research, writing, and communication abilities. Extremely organized and detail-oriented. Experience in program planning, new student orientations, and proofreading.

✔ Secondary school teacher with NCATE certification in English and History. Experienced in curriculum development, classroom management, and student evaluations. Professional, ethical, and committed to student learning.

24. Keywords Are Winning Words

Keywords are part of the foundation of a successful resume. These words enable you to communicate your competency, qualifications, and achievements in persuasive language.

The following list of keywords is designed to jumpstart your thinking about your own keyword list—a list that is specific to your career, industry, and objective.

Profession	Keywords	
Accounting	Accounts payable	General ledger
	Accounts receivable	Internal controls
	Auditing	Process improvement
	Cost reduction	Project accounting
	CPA	Project costing
	Due diligence	Regulatory compliance
	Financial analysis	Risk management
	Financial reporting	SAP
Banking	Asset management	Mergers and acquisitions
	Commercial lending	Portfolio management
	Consumer credit	Regulatory compliance
	Debt and equity financing	Risk management
	Foreign exchange	
Customer service	Call center operations	Customer retention
	Client relationship management	Help desk operations
		Sales support
	Customer loyalty	Training
Government	Competitive procurement	Fiscal year budgets
	Constituent affairs	Fixed price contracts
	Contract awards and administration	Grant funding and administration
	Request for proposal (RFP)	

Health care	Case management	Hospital administration
	Clinical	Insurance reimbursement
	Community outreach	Provider networks
	Continuity of care	Provider relations
	Healthcare delivery system	Standard of care

Human resources	Benefits	Labor relations
	Campus recruiting/college relations	Manpower planning
	Career transition/ outplacement	Organizational development
	Change management	Needs analysis
	Compensation	Pension plan administration
	EEOC	Talent development and deployment
	Employee recruitment	Training and development
	Employee relations	Workforce optimization
	HRIS (Human Resources Information System)	

International business	Cross-cultural negotiations	New market development
	Due diligence and value analysis	New product launch
	Global marketing and sales	Offshore operations
	Government regulations	Strategic acquisition
	Multinational joint ventures and partnerships	Trade and barrier transactions

Legal	Advocacy	Intellectual capital
	Appeal	LexisNexis
	Arbitration	Liability
	Case law	Litigation
	Client representation	Mediation
	Defense strategy	Negotiations
	Deposition	Plaintiff
	Document preparation	Third-party payors

Manufacturing	Capacity planning and optimization Continuous process improvement Ergonomic efficiency Facilities planning and maintenance ISO 9000 Just-in-Time Labor relations Line supervision	Manufacturing operations Multi-site operations management Operations management Production yield Productivity Reengineering Quality assurance Quality control
Marketing	Account management Brand strategy Competitive pricing Cross-functional marketing teams Focus groups Global marketing and business development Market research and data analysis	Multimedia marketing communications Product design and launch Product positioning Product reengineering Strategic alliances and partnerships Web design
Public relations	Account management Advertising communications Business development Campaign management Client relationships Creative services Crisis communications Community affairs/relations Government affairs Investor and shareholder relations	Media placements Media relations Press releases Promotions Public affairs Sales promotions Special events Sponsorships

Real estate	Asset growth and management	Historic preservation/ landmarks
	Asset workout and recovery	Investment valuation
	Bids and proposals	Investor presentations and funding
	Commercial leasing	
	Competitive bidding	Portfolio management
	Construction management	Property management
	Development projects	Turnkey operations

Sales	Closing skills	National account management
	Competitive market share	New business development
	Consultative selling	Presentations
	Cross-selling	Product lifecycle
	Customer relationship management	Promotions and incentives
	Customer satisfaction	Sales training
	Key accounts	Solution selling
		Team management

Teaching	Classroom management	Instructional materials
	Continuing education	Subject matter expert
	Curriculum design	Student counseling, mentoring, and tutoring
	Educational administration	

25. What Can You Do for Us? The Power of Accomplishments

Competence, like truth, beauty and contact lenses,
is in the eye of the beholder.

Laurence J. Peter, *The Peter Principle*

From an employer's point of view, there is no greater predictor of success than past performance. To convince potential employers that you are the best candidate for the job, you must be able to clearly articulate and sell your accomplishments.

1. Start by writing one-line statements about various aspects of your experiences (in school, at work, and through community/professional activities). Use your resume checklists to organize your thoughts.

2. Convert each activity into an accomplishment statement. Accomplishment statements usually begin with an action verb, describe your activities, and end with a statement of what you achieved.

   Examples:

   - Reduced operating expenses by 25% by improving efficiency and decreasing expenses.
   - Selected new vendors for office services, resulting in improved customer service and satisfaction.
   - Generated $50,000 in new sales during first twelve months.
   - Created media relations campaign for health care provider, resulting in story placements in three major metropolitan newspapers.

3. Make your list of accomplishment statements as comprehensive as possible. You can always make editorial changes later.

4. After you have completed your list, edit the statements to use the most powerful verbiage and reflect tangible evidence of results.

5. If you are using a chronological resume format, make sure that you list each accomplishment directly beneath the company where you acquired it.

6. If you are using a functional resume, you will need to group related accomplishments together under functional headings (regardless of when and where you accomplished those results).

7. Finally, review your accomplishment statements in the context of your specific job objective; then organize and present the statements in order of their relevance to the potential employer.

26. Sample Resumes

The first two resumes, both for Janet Smith, illustrate how the same job hunter can use different resume styles to create different perceptions of her qualifications and experience. The following five resumes showcase people with a variety of career types.

Chronological

JANET SMITH
1055 West Columbia Avenue
Chicago, Illinois 60626
Ph: (773) 761-3185
e-mail: jsmith@fauxmail.com

PROFILE

Highly motivated real estate executive with strong leadership, portfolio management, and business development experience. Ability to develop creative synergies between strategy, processes, and people. Strong financial management, forecasting, and problem-solving capabilities.

PROFESSIONAL EXPERIENCE

3/99–
5/04
Grubb & Ellis Management Services, Inc., Chicago, Illinois
Vice President, Portfolio Manager
Special competence in managing to a yield; P&L responsibility, computer modeling, client interface, budget responsibility, financial management, profit improvement, quality control, staff development, and marketing
- Portfolio revenue of $12 million
- Responsible for over $100 million in assets totaling 1.3 million dollars
- Prepare proposals and presentation materials used for procurement of new business
- Consistently in top 10% in expense control
- Coordinated capital improvement projects over $3 million

1/92–
2/99
PM Realty Group, Chicago, Illinois
District Manager, Southfield, Michigan 7/98–2/99
- Generated district revenue of $14.3 million
- Directed district property management for 1.2 million square feet of office and retail properties
- Directed the professional staff of seven properties in four cities
- Created marketing programs for all properties
- Coordinated and implemented all aspects of property takeovers

Senior Property Manager, Chicago, Illinois 2/97–6/98
- Reduced operating expense .53 per square foot
- Collected $96,000 of past due rent in the first 30 days
- Developed and maintained client relationships
- Planned, coordinated, and monitored all construction phases for tenant and building improvements
- Prepared and monitored annual property budget

page two
Resume of Janet Smith

General Manager 1/95–2/97

- Reduced expenses .20/sf during the first year
- Managed prestigious suburban commercial property
- Supervised accounting functions, prepared budgets, escalations, cash projections, financials
- Promoted good tenant relations through effective management
- Enhanced value of property by increasing net operating expenses

Property Manager 1/92–12/94

- Managed 565,000 square feet of North Michigan Avenue commercial/ retail properties
- Increased NOI by $250,000 while increasing services and efficiency
- Organized cash management, leasing and marketing activities, tenant relations, contract negotiation
- Prepared annual operating budget, cash projections, and monthly reports
- Developed tenant reimbursement program for additional rent – 100% recovery
- Coordinated tenant build-outs and capital improvements

AFFILIATIONS

Board Member: University of Chicago Women's Business Group

EDUCATION

University of Chicago, MBA 1998
Mundelein College, Bachelor of Arts, 1991
CPM, RPA, Licensed Illinois Real Estate Broker

Functional

JANET SMITH

1055 West Columbia Avenue
Chicago, Illinois 60626
Ph: (773) 761-3185
E-mail: jsmith@fauxmail.com

PROFILE

Visionary leader with strong strategic planning, finance, and management abilities. Risk taker with excellent creative problem solving, organization, and communication skills. Knowledgeable in business development, financial analysis, asset management, real estate, and project management.

EDUCATION

University of Chicago, MBA, 1998, The Executive Program (XP-66)

Mundelein College, Bachelor of Arts, 1991

EXPERTISE

Leadership/Strategic Thinker

Created and developed concept for Mobile Screening Technologies, Inc.: researched industry; developed pro forma; wrote business plan, financial package, and marketing plan; outlined investment strategy; initiated management team; developed Executive Board of Directors; searched for investment financing.

Provided leadership to expansive organization at Grubb & Ellis and PM Realty Group by developing objectives, strategies, programs, projects, and activities for more than 45 different real estate assets that consistently met or exceeded all financial hurdles.

- Special competence in managing to a yield with responsibility for more than $150 million in assets totaling 1.3 million SF; P&L responsibility for Portfolio revenue of $12 million, NOI of $8 million; coordinated capital improvement projects of more than $3 million.

- Directed district property management for 1.2 million SF of office and retail properties and the professional staff of seven properties in four cities; responsible for district profitability— generated district revenue of $14.3 million, NOI of $2.7 million at PM Realty Group.

- Coordinated and implemented all aspects of property takeovers and the repositioning of troubled assets.

Analytical/Finance

- Created plans to reduce debt on troubled assets. Successful in forecasting financial accomplishments, industry trends, and market status.

- Developed and prepared more than 150 different budget packages, which included pro forma, operation budget, capital budget, 5-year plans, narratives, cost analysis, and all accompanying schedules.

- Prepared and analyzed monthly and year-end financial statements.

- Experience managing to a yield. Profit improvement consistently in top 10% in expense control.

Communication

- Wrote business plan, marketing plan, and financial package for new business concept for Mobile Screening Technologies, Inc.

- Marketing and Sales Presentation development and execution to institutional and private investors culminating in new business valued at more than $250,000 annually.

Page 2

JANET SMITH

Management
- Managed more than 45 diverse (office, building management, engineering, security, accounting, leasing) staffs and achieved mission and goals of the organization which resulted in higher revenue, decreased operating costs, and continued increased net operating income.
- Defined and identified challenges and impediments to success. Created and developed plans of action to correct defects, implement plans, and follow through to completion.

PROFESSIONAL WORK HISTORY

2004 to Present	Mobile Screening Technologies, Inc., Chicago, Illinois President/CEO
1999 to 2004	Grubb & Ellis Management Services, Inc., Chicago, Illinois Vice President, Portfolio Manager
1987 to 1994	PM Realty Group, Chicago, Illinois District Manager Southfield, Michigan 1998–1999 General Manager Chicago, Illinois 1995–1997

LICENSES AND CERTIFICATIONS

Institute of Real Estate Management (IREM), CPM—1993

Licensed Illinois Real Estate Broker since 1991
Building Owners and Managers Association (BOMA), RPA—1989

COMMUNITY ACTIVITIES

Past Board Member: University of Chicago Women's Business Group
Past Vice Chairman BOMA Chicago Education Committee
Past Board Member: Holy Family Hospital Women's Board
Past Board Member: St. Mary's Women's Board

SANDRA GRADUATE

5150 Laramie Avenue
Cleveland, Ohio 44444
550-555-1111
sgrad24@fauxmail.com

OBJECTIVE

Entry-level accounting job in public accounting firm.

EDUCATION

B.S. in Accounting   Expected May 2005

Case Western Reserve University, Cleveland, Ohio

GPA 3.6/4.0

Relevant Course Work:

Financial Accounting	Cost Accounting
Auditing	Federal Taxation
Corporate Finance	Information Systems

WORK EXPERIENCE

Accounting Intern   May–August 2003

MTR and Associates, Akron, Ohio

- Reviewed and corrected accounting entries.
- Assisted with financial planning and analysis.
- Identified $25,000 in billing errors.
- Wrote reports.

Accounts Receivables Clerk   1999–2001

Johnson & Smith, Cleveland, Ohio

- Collected past-due balances.

JOHN Q. FOODY

555 South Michigan Avenue, Chicago, IL 60605
Ph. (312) 461-1666 Cell: (312) 555-1234
E-mail: jqfood@fauxmail.com

PROFILE

General management and marketing executive with
successful track record in new business start-up, strategic planning, marketing,
and organizational development. Extensive background in food industry.

PROFESSIONAL EXPERIENCE

FOOD PRODUCTS UNLIMITED, CHICAGO, IL 1996–present

General Manager (1999–2004)

- Managed profit and loss responsibility for a $30 million company.
- Repositioned the business from a commodity to a value-added, solution-oriented branded manufacturer.
- Doubled revenues in five-year period.
- Achieved 200% increase in premium branded food-based business.

Vice President, Marketing (1996–1999)

- Directed all marketing, new product development, marketing research, and marketing communications efforts.
- Managed 10 people and a development budget of $4 million.
- Repositioned branded products for new target market.
- Grew major business lines by 150% in the first two years.

THE COOK'S CORNER, CHICAGO, IL 1991–1996

Vice President of Marketing and New Business Ventures

- Directed competitive analysis, created market positioning and entry strategy, and developed business plans for a new business segment, resulting in $10 million in new revenues during first two years.
- Designed and implemented a direct mail campaign that increased sales by 25%.

Resume of **John Q. Foody**
Page two

KRB PRODUCTS, CHICAGO, IL   1982–1991

Marketing Director

- Managed a four-person department with a $3 million budget.
- Managed new product development and product launch strategies for three new products lines, resulting in $200 million in sales.
- Directed national advertising and public relations programs that won international awards.
- Initiated a public relations strategy that doubled company visibility in the trade media.

EDUCATION

Loyola University, Chicago, IL, 1982
Master of Business Administration — Marketing concentration

Loyola University, Chicago, IL, 1978
Bachelor's of Science in Business

HONORS AND AWARDS

Excellence in Design Award, International Association of Design Executives, 1995

PROFESSIONAL ACTIVITIES

Board Member, International Food Executives Group (2000–2002)

Samuel Salesman, Jr.

111 Sales Drive
Milwaukee, WI 77777
Ph.: 777-777-7777
E-mail: Samsalesjr@fauxmail.com

PROFILE

Seasoned sales and marketing executive with extensive experience in retail and consumer industries. Strong negotiating, problem-solving, and customer service skills. Knowledgeable in small business management, human resources, business planning, and distribution.

PROFESSIONAL EXPERIENCE

1991–present   **SS & Son, Milwaukee, WI**

President/CEO	(2003–present)
Vice President/Partner	(1994–2003)
Sales Manager	(1991–1994)

Lead and manage company that supplies gardening and lawn supplies to wholesalers and retailers. Increased revenues by 20–25% annually.

Redesigned products in order to reduce costs, increase efficiency, and respond to customer needs.

Review financial statements and identify sales trends; coordinate and facilitate monthly sales meetings.

Manage sales representatives in five-state territory.

1981–1990   **Fred's Wholesale Supply, St. Louis, MO**
Sales Manager

Managed 10–12 sales representative in multi-state territory; drove and maintained sales of $3 million annually.

Compiled regional reports for main office.

EDUCATION

University of St. Louis
    Major: Business   1979–1981

ARLENE S. HIRSCH

431 South Dearborn #1202
Chicago, IL 60605
(312) 461-1065
ASHirsch@aol.com
Web site: www.arlenehirsch.com

PROFILE

Dynamic, creative, and resourceful career consultant knowledgeable in career change, career development, transition management, emotional intelligence, resilience, and job search. Strong teaching, writing, and communication skills.

PROFESSIONAL EXPERIENCE

1983–Present   Arlene S. Hirsch and Associates, Chicago, IL
Career and Psychological Counseling
Principal

- Developed and maintain career and psychological counseling practice providing individual counseling to adults with career concerns.

- Provide individual and group outplacement services to corporations. Assist with resume writing, job search strategies, and interviewing techniques. Corporate clients include Aon, AT&T, Baxter Healthcare, Caremark, and Chicago Tribune.

- Present seminars and workshops on work-related topics to a variety of government and non-profit organizations, including American Medical Association, Career Transition Center, Chicago Bar Association, and the FBI.

- Authored several best-selling career books in collaboration with the Wall Street Journal.

- Wrote weekly column for StartupJournal.com and numerous articles for CareerJournal.com.

- Designed and delivered online career courses for Dow Jones University, Barnes & Noble University, P&G Career Center, and PowerEd.com.

- Piloted career planning program for Lake Forest Graduate School of Management Executive MBA program.

- Participated in rollout of career planning program for Motorola University.

- Coordinated regional career counseling program for the Nuclear Regulatory Commission.

- Appeared on radio and television to discuss career and work-related topics, including CNBC, ABC, WGN, WBEZ, and WFYR.

Page two

ARLENE S. HIRSCH

1976–1978   Panter, Nelson & Bernfield, Ltd., Chicago, IL
             Office Manager

- Managed 50-person corporate law firm.

- Hired, trained, supervised, and evaluated clerical staff.

- Purchased equipment and supplies.

- Coordinated office relocation to larger space.

- Worked with architect and interior designer to plan new space.

- Administered employee benefits programs.

EDUCATION

Northwestern University, Evanston, IL
  M.A., Counseling Psychology, 1983
  Externship: Catholic Charities Family Counseling Center
  Practicum: Jewish Vocational Service

University of Iowa, Iowa City, IA
  B.A., English and Secondary Education, 1973
  Internship: West High School, Iowa City, IA
  9th and 10th grade Honors English classes

BOOKS

Hirsch, Arlene S. *How to Be Happy at Work* (Second Edition), JIST Publishing, Indianapolis, IN, 2003.

Hirsch, Arlene S. *Love Your Work and Success Will Follow*, John Wiley and Sons, New York, NY, 1996.

Hirsch, Arlene S. *The Wall Street Journal Premier Guide to Interviewing* (Third Edition), John Wiley and Sons, New York, NY, 1998.

Hirsch, Arlene S. *The Wall Street Journal Premier Guide to Interviewing* (Second Edition), John Wiley and Sons, New York, NY, 1996.

Hirsch, Arlene S. *The Wall Street Journal Premier Guide to Interviewing*, John Wiley and Sons, New York, NY, 1994.

Hirsch, Arlene S. *VGM's Careers Checklists*, VGM Career Horizons, Lincolnwood, IL, 1990.

KENNETH CREATIVE

8750 Kaycee Drive
Kansas City, KS 63115
(444) 362-1234
kc@fauxmail.com

PROFESSIONAL OBJECTIVE

Challenging position in marketing communications, public relations, or special
events management.

ACCOMPLISHMENTS

Marketing

▶ Designed and implemented creative sales and marketing strategies
to capitalize on consumer trends and penetrate new markets.

▶ Recruited, trained, and supervised marketing coordinator and
assistant.

▶ Developed direct-mail marketing campaign that generated
$200,000 in new business.

▶ Worked with consultant to develop and implement company
Web site.

Public Relations

▶ Developed and implemented public relations campaign for
philanthropic organization, resulting in major media placements
and fund-raising events.

▶ Coordinated two charity auctions that raised $150,000 for community development fund.

▶ Wrote press releases and compiled media kits that were distributed to all major newspapers and magazines.

▶ Generated two major corporate sponsorships to sponsor annual
charity race.

Page two

KENNETH CREATIVE

WORK EXPERIENCE

| 1998–present | Financial Executives Forum, Kansas City, MO |
| | Event Planner |

1994–1998   FRC Consulting Company, Overland Park, KS
Marketing Coordinator

1992–1994   PR Agency, Inc., Bloomfield, KS
Assistant Account Manager

COMMUNITY ACTIVITIES

Rotary Club International

Botanical Gardens

Public Relations Society of America

United Way

EDUCATION

University of Kansas, Lawrence, KS
B.S. Communications, 1992

27. Resume Planner

He who fails to plan plans to fail.

Anonymous

I created this checklist to help you assemble the information that you need to plan, organize, and write your resume. Use an extra sheet of paper if you need more space.

WORK HISTORY

List your previous jobs in reverse chronological order (beginning with your most recent job).

Name of employer/company: _____

Employer address: _____

Telephone: _____

Fax: _____

Web site: _____

Supervisor's name, title, telephone, and e-mail address: _____

_____

Dates of employment: _____

Job title: _____

Responsibilities (use your job description, if necessary): _____

_____

Specific accomplishments: _____

_____

Skills used: _____

On-the-job training: _____

References: _____

_____

Name of employer/company: _____

Employer address: _____

Telephone: _____

Fax: _____

Web site: _____

Supervisor's name, title, telephone, and e-mail address: _____

_____

Dates of employment: _____

Job title: _____

Responsibilities (use your job description, if necessary): _____

_____

Specific accomplishments: _____

_____

Skills used: _____

On-the-job training: _____

References: _____

_____

Name of employer/company: _____

Employer address: _____

Telephone: _____

Fax: _____

Web site: _____

Supervisor's name, title, telephone, and e-mail address: _____

_____

Dates of employment: _____

Job title: _____

Responsibilities (use your job description, if necessary): _____

_____

Specific accomplishments: _____

_____

Skills used: _____

On-the-job training: _____

References: _____

_____

EDUCATION

Name of college/university: _____

Location (city and state): _____

Dates attended: _____

Degree(s): _____

Major(s): _____

Minor(s): _____

Areas of concentration/related courses: _____

Internships/work-study programs: _____

Extracurricular activities: _____

Special projects: _____

Honors and awards: _____

COMMUNITY/VOLUNTEER ACTIVITIES

Name of organization: _____

Location of organization: _____

Dates of services: _____

Title or office held: _____

Activities: _____

Accomplishments: _____

HONORS AND AWARDS

Title of honor/award: _____

Date received: _____

Purpose of award: _____

Name of granting institution: _____

LICENSES OR CERTIFICATES

Name of license/certificate: _____

Date received: _____

Granting institution: _____

28. Cover Letters: Why You Need Them

Every time you send out a resume, you must include a customized cover letter. To skip this part of the process is to label yourself as lazy, uncaring, and unprofessional.

A cover letter has many goals and purposes:

1. To introduce you to future employers
2. To ensure that your resume makes it into the right hands
3. To showcase your writing skills
4. To present your qualifications
5. To sell yourself
6. To make a good first impression
7. To demonstrate your professionalism

29. How to Wreck a Cover Letter

Nothing is more terrible than ignorance in action.

Johann von Goethe

1. Spell the name of the company and/or the recruiter incorrectly.

2. Send the letter with your resume to the wrong address.

3. Do not address the letter to anyone specifically by name.

4. Don't worry about typos or spelling errors. Anyone can use spell check.

5. Don't bother putting your contact information on the letter because it's on your resume anyway.

6. Address the letter to "Dear Sir."

7. Don't worry about the attachments—you can always send them later.

8. Express your creativity and originality with brightly colored paper and unique color combinations and typefaces.

9. Use the reader's first name to demonstrate that you are comfortable with authority, even if you've never met him or her before.

10. Don't bother finding out the addressee's title and position; no one cares about those things.

11. Write like you talk—don't be afraid to use slang or cool phrases. It's important for them to know you're cool.

12. Don't use brand-new paper and envelopes. You wouldn't want the potential employer to think that you are desperate or really want the position.

30. Rules of the Cover-Letter-Writing Road

There are no shortcuts to any place worth going.

Beverly Sills

1. Invest in high-quality paper and envelopes (ideally, they'll match the stock of your resume) as well as a good printer.

2. Address your letter to a specific person by name and title. Double-check to make sure that you are spelling their name and title correctly.

3. When in doubt, err on the side of formality by using the words "Mr.", "Ms.", "Mrs.", "Dr.", or "Professor."

4. Make sure that your letter is grammatically perfect and error free.

5. Personalize your communication by writing it in your own words. You never want your letter to sound as if someone else has written it.

6. Use the first paragraph to introduce yourself. Tell the reader why you are writing and how you heard about them.

7. Show that you know something about the company and the industry. This is where your research comes in. Don't go overboard—just make it clear that you didn't pick this company out of the phone book. You know who they are and what they do and *you* have chosen them.

8. Use terms, phrases, and keywords that are meaningful to the employer. If necessary, review Checklist 24 for ideas.

9. Identify those qualifications and accomplishments that are most relevant to the employer's needs and build the body of the letter around a discussion of your qualifications and experience *as they pertain to the company's needs.*

10. If you have relevant experience or accomplishments that are not listed on your resume, be sure to include them in your cover letter.

11. Always refer the reader to your resume for further information and encourage them to contact you as well.

12. When e-mailing your cover letter, brevity is even more important. The nature of e-mail calls for concise communication, in part because it's harder to read on-screen than on paper. You should be able to write a convincing cover letter in a few brief paragraphs.

13. Never mention money unless specifically asked—and then provide as few details as possible. Instead, tell the hiring manager that you would be happy to discuss your salary history and requirements during the interview.

14. Always include current contact information (include your cell phone number and e-mail address, if appropriate), even if that information has already been included on your resume. Sometimes the resumes and cover letters get separated from each other.

15. Let the reader know (politely) what you would like to happen next—for example, you would like them to call you in for an interview or you would like to send them your portfolio.

16. Sign off with a traditional ending, such as Yours truly, Truly yours, or Sincerely. Save your Ciaos, Adioses, and Later, Dudes for your family and friends.

31. Cover Letter Greatness

Good, better, best; never let it rest till your good is better and your better is best.

Unknown

Most people don't take the time to write dynamite cover letters that lift them head and shoulders above the competition. When you understand the basics of cover letter writing, it isn't that much more effort to write really great cover letters. Here's how:

1. If you attended a prestigious university or worked for a pedigree (Fortune 100) company, include that information early in the cover letter in order to establish credibility and respect.

2. If you have a good networking contact (referral source), make sure that you do some legitimate "name-dropping" in order to establish a friendlier (potentially more informal) tone.

3. Don't be afraid to toot your own horn, but don't overdo it. The key here is to identify and elaborate on specific skills and accomplishments that will impress—and potentially be useful to—the hiring manager.

4. Put words in other people's mouths. In other words, use quotes from your references (with their permission, of course) that reflect some special dimensions of your character and work ethic.

5. Don't be afraid to be original. When it comes to cover letters, a little creativity goes far. For example, you might try creating two columns in your letter to demonstrate how precisely you meet the employer's requirements:

Your requirements	My qualifications
5 years retail sales experience	6 years as sales associate and sales manager for Bloomingdales

6. End the letter with a postscript (P.S.) that includes some relevant or interesting information for the reader to mull over. Because almost everyone reads the postscript (even if they don't read the letter), you have one last chance to make an indelible impression.

32. Cover Letter Worksheet

Writing is easy. All you do is stare at a blank sheet of paper until drops of blood form on your forehead.

Gene Fowler

Name of company: _____

Name of contact person: _____

Title of contact person: _____

Address: _____

E-mail address: _____

Web site (for research): _____

Job title: _____

How you heard about the position: _____

Name of referral (if any): _____

Relationship to referral (if any): _____

Why you are interested in this company/position: _____

Major selling points: _____

_____

Follow-up notes: _____

_____

_____

_____

33. Sample Cover Letters

The best way to have a good idea is to have lots of ideas.

Linus Pauling

Samuel Smith
655 West Irving Park
Any Town, Any State 00087
Telephone: (414) 679-0743

September 15, 2004

Mr. John Doe, Director of Human Resources
Any Company Intl.
111 North Any Street
Any City, State 99976

Dear Mr. Doe:

I am interested in responding to your September 14, 2004 advertisement in the Sun-Times for a Pharmaceutical Sales Representative.

Your ad indicates that you are looking for a self-motivated and highly energetic college graduate with good communication skills and an interest in science. As you can see from the enclosed resume, I graduated from the University of Pennsylvania in June 2004 with a bachelor's degree in biology and a GPA of 3.5/4.0 in my major.

Throughout my college career, I worked in retail sales positions in order to support myself and pay for my college tuition. As an assistant sales manager at The Gap, I consistently met and exceeded my sales goals and was often recruited to train new sales associates. As one young customer commented, "I wish all of the salespeople here were more like you. You are always so helpful!"

At this point in my career, I would like to combine my acumen for sales with my scientific interest and knowledge. I am aware that your company has many outstanding products in the pharmaceutical industry and I am confident that I could represent your organization effectively.

Thank you for your time and consideration. I look forward to hearing from you.

Sincerely,

Samuel Smith

Samuel Smith
Enclosure

Jane Socialworker
4545 East Boulevard
Cincinnati OH 46534
Ph: (674) 654-2345
Email: jane4545@fauxmail.com

April 12, 2004

Ms. May Bloom
Director of Social Services
Northeastern Community Services
2341 South Western Avenue
Cincinnati, OH 46534

Dear Ms. Bloom,

Natalie Fox recommended that I contact you regarding a clinical social work position. I first met Natalie when she and I worked together at Travelers Aid and Immigration, where she often raved about the community programs that you and your staff have developed for at-risk youth.

During the four years that I worked at Travelers Aid, I provided outreach, crisis intervention, and group counseling to troubled youths. My clinical training at the University of Chicago prepared me well for this work and has enabled me to work well with this difficult population. I also have extensive experience with a diverse range of psychological disorders.

In my most recent performance evaluation, my current supervisor described me as "highly intelligent, competent, compassionate, honest, and kind." I believe these are the qualities that enable me to work so effectively with all kinds of clients and populations.

The enclosed resume will further describe my qualifications. If you would like to schedule an interview, please contact me.

Sincerely,

Jane Socialworker

Jane Socialworker
Enclosure

P.S. Natalie says that it's your turn to buy her lunch!

Thomas Teacher
3412 Fairview Lane
Skokie, IL 60076
(847) 222-2222
tomteacher@fauxmail.com

March 18, 2004

Dr. Phillip Principal
Principal
Prairie View School
3216 Prairie View Road
Skokie, IL 60076

Dear Dr. Principal:

My son Jason suggested that I contact you regarding the opening for a middle school teacher at Prairie View School. Jason is a fifth grader at Prairie View and, through him, I have grown to respect and admire both the teachers and the administration at the school. I would love to be able to contribute my talents to your organization.

As you can see from the enclosed resume, I am an experienced middle school teacher who has taught seventh and eighth grade English and History. I am NCATE certified in secondary education.

I have excellent classroom management skills and am comfortable working with an established curriculum or designing new classroom materials. I bring a great deal of energy and enthusiasm to my teaching, which I know my students enjoy and appreciate. Through the years, many former students have told me, "Mr. Teacher, you've always been my favorite teacher."

Thank you in advance for your interest. I look forward to hearing from you.

Sincerely,

Thomas Teacher

Thomas Teacher
Enclosure

34. Cover Letter Template

Efficiency is doing better what is already being done.

Peter F. Drucker

Having made the argument for creativity and originality on previous pages, I'm also including a cover letter template to help you with basic cover letter format. After completing the first draft of your cover letter from the template below, you need to review and revise it to make it distinctive and impressive.

Your name: _____

Your address: _____

City: _____

State: _____

Zip: _____

Home phone: _____

Work phone: _____

E-mail address: _____

Date: _____

Person's name: _____

Title: _____

Agency or organization name: _____

Street address: _____

City: _____

State: _____

Zip: _____

Dear: _____

Paragraph 1

I would like to apply for the position of _____.

Paragraph 2

My relevant experience for the position includes

1. _____

2. _____

3. _____

4. _____

5. _____

Paragraph 3

I believe that I would be an asset to your organization because

1. _____

2. _____

3. _____

4. _____

5. _____

Paragraph 4

The enclosed resume further describes my qualifications. Please contact me if you have any additional questions or would like to schedule an interview. Thank you for your time and consideration. I look forward to your response.

Sincerely,

Signature

Typed Name

Enclosure

A-Job-Hunting We Will Go

Conducting a successful job search takes both skill and art. To get to the art, you need to know how to identify job leads, network effectively, and join forces with employment agencies and recruiters.

35. Testing Your Readiness IQ

*A lot of fellows nowadays have a B.A., M.D., or Ph.D.
Unfortunately, they don't have a J.O.B.*

"Fats" Domino

There's more to successful job hunting than blindly sending out resumes and cover letters. To assess whether you are ready to launch a good job search campaign, rate your responses to the statements below according to the following scale:

1 = strongly agree   2 = agree   3 = not sure   4 = disagree   5 = no way!

_____ 1. I can identify my strongest skills and abilities.

_____ 2. I know—and can articulate—my best accomplishments.

_____ 3. I understand my interests and how they fit into my career goals.

_____ 4. I know what I need to do to be motivated and excel in a job.

_____ 5. I understand my values and priorities.

_____ 6. I have an achievable career objective.

_____ 7. I understand what skills employers are seeking in candidates.

_____ 8. I know what skills I have to offer these employers.

_____ 9. I can clearly explain to employers what I do well and enjoy doing.

_____ 10. I have support (family, friends, mentors) for the change I want to make.

_____ 11. I know how to use the Internet to conduct research on occupations and employers.

_____ 12. I can identify potential employers that I want to contact.

_____ 13. I can develop a network of people that I can contact for referrals and job leads.

_____ 14. I have a strategy to contact my network.

_____ 15. I can use the telephone to develop prospects and get referrals and interviews.

_____ 16. I can plan and implement an effective direct-mail job search campaign.

_____ 17. I have written my resume in accordance with my job objective.

_____ 18. I have prepared a sample cover letter.

_____ 19. I know how to generate job interviews.

_____ 20. I have developed responses to typical interview questions.

_____ 21. I can anticipate and respond to illegal questions.

_____ 22. I have a strategy to deal with my weaknesses and liabilities.

_____ 23. I have created a list of stories or examples as illustrations of my skills and strengths.

_____ 24. I can follow up on job interviews.

_____ 25. I have a strategy to negotiate salary and compensation packages.

_____ Total

Add your ratings for a total composite score. If you score 50 points or less, you are prepared to start your search. If your total score is 51 points or more, you need to work on developing your job hunting skills.

Based on your responses, list the skills you need to develop in order to increase your job search readiness:

1. _____

2. _____

3. _____

4. _____

5. _____

6. _____

7. _____

8. _____

9. _____

10. _____

36. Job Hunting While Still Employed

*It's not so much that we're afraid of change or so in love with the
old ways, but it's that place in between that we fear. . . .
It's like being between trapezes. It's Linus when his blanket is in
the dryer. There's nothing to hold on to.*

Marilyn Ferguson

Conventional wisdom has always maintained that it's easier to find a new job while
you're still employed. Like much conventional wisdom, that's only partly true. While it
may make it easier for you to pay your bills, it isn't always easy to find the time or energy
to conduct a good search. Here are some guidelines that you can use to incorporate a job
search into an already hectic schedule.

1. Make your job search a priority. Although you obviously cannot devote entire days
   to looking for a new job, you can work every day toward the goal of finding a new
   job. If you can find a way to carve out 30 to 40 minutes per day for job search
   activities, it will help you sustain your motivation and persist in your efforts.

2. Take time to engage in some meaningful self-assessment before you start barnstorm-
   ing the job market. To facilitate that goal, use the checklists in Section 1, take some
   vocational tests, and, if necessary, find yourself a good career counselor who can
   help you clarify your goals and direction.

3. Write your resume with your job objective in mind. Use the Internet to research
   potential employers and identify open positions which match up with your goals.

4. Develop a networking strategy that you feel comfortable with. Because you are still
   employed, you need to think carefully about who you can trust with the knowledge
   of your job search, as you don't want the information that you are job hunting leak-
   ing back to your current employer.

5. Use common sense and good judgment. Don't read the classified ads at your desk
   or leave your resume in the photocopy machine. Do bring your cell phone to work
   and use it to make and receive calls during your lunch hour and on your break, but
   be careful to safeguard your privacy. You don't want anyone to overhear your conversations.

6. Set up networking meetings and interviews before or after work or during your lunch hour. However, if you are normally a casual-dress person, suddenly starting to wear suits to work is going to send a red flag to the people you work with.

7. Don't ignore your current job responsibilities. They are also a priority. Even though your heart isn't in it, don't develop a bad attitude or turn out slipshod work. The key is to balance your job search priorities with your job responsibilities so that neither one suffers too much.

8. Be realistic about how long it takes to move from one job to another. Because you are still employed, your job search will inevitability take longer than you want it to. This is the compromise that you accepted when you elected to stay in your current job. If you work steadily toward your goal of finding a new job and stay motivated, energized, and optimistic, the process will be less frustrating and ultimately more successful.

37. Seven Job Search Myths

The closest to perfection a person ever comes is when he fills out a job application form.

Stanley J. Randall

When it comes to job hunting, there is no shortage of "experts" to tell you exactly what you need to do to find a good job. That said, there's also no limit to the amount of bad advice you can accumulate in the process of your search. Here is a list of some of the most common job hunting myths.

Myth #1: There is one right way to find a job.

Although many job hunting surveys point to the power of networking as the single most valuable job search strategy, an effective job search strategy is much like a well-built financial portfolio that reflects the value of diversification. In addition to networking, make sure that you respond to advertised listings, talk to recruiters, contact potential employers directly, and learn how to parlay contract or temporary jobs into permanent full-time positions.

Myth #2: If a job isn't advertised in the paper or on the company's Web site, there aren't any positions available.

Although many employers use classified ads and online job postings to advertise open positions, many jobs are never advertised. In order to identify these hidden jobs, you must proactively call companies that interest you and continue to develop and expand your network of contacts.

Myth #3: Nobody reads cover letters.

As a matter of course, resumes should almost always be accompanied by a well-written cover letter. This cover letter can be valuable for several reasons:

- It targets a specific person and job title as a way of ensuring that your resume makes it to the desk of the right hiring authority
- It provides an opportunity to highlight those skills and experiences that are most relevant to your target (regardless of whether they are listed on your resume)

- It is a clear illustration of your writing skills
- It is the professional thing to do

Myth #4: A resume should always be one page.

As traditional career ladders have vanished, so too has the one-page resume started to go the way of the dinosaur. For many experienced job hunters, limiting your resume to one page doesn't make sense if that means that you must also eliminate potentially important information in the process. As a general rule, your resume should be succinct and well written. Depending on the nature of your experience, you may need two pages to include all relevant information. Having said that, try to include the most relevant information in the first page.

Myth #5: If a company likes my resume, they will call me in for an interview.

In a perfect world, this would be the reality of every job search. But in the so-called Information Age, the reality is that it's easy for your resume to get lost among the hordes of paperwork. It is incumbent on you to make sure that your resume gets noticed. You can do that by following up your resume and cover letter with a telephone call or e-mail to make sure that the recruiter knows who you are and why you are so well qualified.

Myth #6: It's not what you know that matters; it's who you know that counts.

In fact, it's both who and what you know that counts. While a good referral can get you in the door and in front of the right people, if you don't have the skills and experience to do the job, the odds are against you. To make sure that doesn't happen, take the time to develop a focused job search strategy that really capitalizes on your strengths and qualifications.

Myth #7: When it comes to sending out resumes, the more the merrier.

Although many people do take a shotgun approach to job hunting, a qualitative approach to the job market is usually more successful than a quantitative one. To do this, you must spend some time and effort researching the job market and identifying specific employers who can benefit from what you have to offer and then approach them, knowledge in hand.

38. Company Research

*You got to be careful if you don't know where you're going,
because you might not get there.*

Yogi Berra

Before you send out a resume and cover letter or go to an interview, you need to research your target organization. Here are a few of the things that you should keep in mind with regard to research.

✔ It is generally easier to find information about a publicly owned company than privately owned companies.

✔ If your target company is publicly owned, you can find the stock price listings on the Web sites of the three major stock exchanges where stock of public companies is traded: the American Stock Exchange (www.amex.com), the New York Stock Exchange (www.nyse.com), and the NASDAQ Stock Market (www.nasdaq.com).

✔ If the target company is a subsidiary or a division of a larger corporation, you can find the name of the parent corporation through Standard & Poors or Dun & Bradstreet.

✔ If the company is privately owned, finding information may be harder. But most companies have their own Web sites where you can learn quite a bit about their organizations. You can also use Google (www.google.com) to conduct a search for any information that has been published about the organization.

✔ You can also find information about companies (both public and private) through directories such as Hoover's (www.hoovers.com). Hoover's is a comprehensive business directory that lists its information online.

✔ For biographical information about top executives, you can use Dun & Bradstreet's *Reference Book of Corporate Managements*. Again, I would recommend that you search for the name of the individual you are interested in with the Google search engine to see if they have written anything or if anything has been written about them.

✔ There is also a wealth of information about companies (and their executives) from the individuals who formerly (or currently) work there. You can usually find some interesting scuttlebutt at the electronic watercooler provided by Vault (www.vault.com).

✔ Professional trade associations also offer a wealth of information and potential networking contacts. If you belong to a professional trade group, review their membership directory to determine whether there is anyone in the group who has worked—or currently works—at the company that interests you. If you don't belong to a group, use the American Society of Association Executives (www.asaenet.org) to determine what groups make the most sense for you.

✔ Finally, don't be afraid to ask the person who contacts you to send you their advertising materials, especially if you are dealing with a small company who may not be that well known.

39. How to Recover from Involuntary Terminations

The shock of unemployment becomes a pathology in its own right.
Robert Farrar Capon

Losing your job—regardless of whether you've been laid off, downsized, right-sized, or terminated for cause—is often a traumatic experience. Here are some steps you can take to help the healing process along:

- ✔ **Acknowledge your worst fears and feelings.** Losing a job is almost always a stressful life event that can fill you with a host of conflicting feelings: anger, anxiety, betrayal, emptiness, guilt, self-doubt. It usually helps to recognize and vent those feelings.

- ✔ **Don't isolate yourself.** This is a time when you are going to need the support of your family, friends, and others. If necessary, seek out the services of a professional career counselor or psychotherapist who can support you during a potentially trying time in your life.

- ✔ **Formulate a game plan.** Develop a plan of action that will allow you to capitalize on your situation by identifying opportunities that match up with your skills, interests, and values.

- ✔ **Familiarize yourself with the skills and tools of job hunting.** If you haven't already done so, review Checklist 35 in order to identify your weaknesses and then formulate a plan of action to develop the job search skills you need in order to be successful.

- ✔ **Try to maintain your perspective.** Although your job loss may feel like a failure to you, it is also an opportunity to learn, grow, and redirect your energies. This is a time when you need to take care of yourself mentally, physically, and spiritually. Use your time wisely to get and stay healthy in every possible way.

- ✔ **Cultivate resilience.** Resilience is the ability to bounce back from setbacks and deal effectively with challenges and obstacles. For most people, this means learning to cultivate a spirit of hope and optimism, connect (or reconnect) with support systems, and develop new skills and game plans. As has often been noted, what doesn't kill you makes you stronger.

40. The Psychological Challenge

*Panic is a sudden desertion of us,
and a going over to the enemy of our imagination.*

Christian Nestell Bovee

Job hunting is taxing under any circumstances. But it is made more complicated by the fact that it often occurs during a time in a person's life when he or she is feeling anxious, insecure, and vulnerable.

✔ Be patient with yourself. It is going to take some time to figure out what you want and to feel comfortable promoting your strengths and (if necessary) discussing your failures and weaknesses. Try to focus on the day-to-day activities rather than the end goal and reward yourself (mentally) when you feel that you have implemented a job search strategy or technique competently.

✔ The Premack Principle in psychology establishes a system of rewards by linking unpleasant tasks to pleasant ones. To make use of this principle in your job search, make certain to reward yourself by doing something that you like to do after you have completed some arguably unpleasant job search task. For example, if you hate to make phone calls but love to go outside and work in the garden, give yourself an hour in the garden for every hour that you spend on the phone making networking calls and setting up interviews.

✔ Learn from your mistakes. Job-hunting skills—like any other skills— require time and practice. Rather than berating yourself every time you say or do something wrong, try to look more objectively at what you might have said and done differently so that you won't make that particular mistake again.

✔ Don't take silence or rejections personally. Job hunting, by its very nature, requires that you suffer through narcissistic injuries on a weekly or even daily basis. Although it may be difficult not to feel hurt when someone doesn't call you back immediately or offer you a job on the spot, it's all part of the "game" of job hunting. Like salespeople who learn to embrace the "no" because it brings them that much closer to the big sale, try to cultivate an attitude of hope and optimism. As psychologist Martin Seligman has noted, "Pessimists may be more realistic, but optimists are more successful and have more fun."

✔ You can't change the big picture, but you can influence your individual situation.

When you focus on the big picture—unemployment rates, labor statistics, and interest rates—it's easy to get overwhelmed by bad news over which you have no control. What you *can* control is your individual situation. By focusing on the people who you can influence, you regain a sense of confidence, self-esteem, and control over your own destiny.

✔ Stay active and involved. Isolation and, by extension, desperation are anathema to successful job hunting. Rather than bury your head in the sand or slink off into a corner to hide in shame, push yourself to become social. Not only will this help your networking efforts, it will also enable you to stay connected to people you care about and those who care about you. Also, consider joining a support group of job hunters who are grappling with similar experiences. That way you can support each other during a period in your lives that may be more stressful than usual.

41. Where the Jobs Are

Find a job you like and you add five days to every week.

H. Jackson Brown, Jr.

A good job search plan is like a diversified portfolio: You need to have lots of different strategies and techniques to identify, create, and land a position. The following overview will help you understand the plethora of options available to you.

1. **Answering help-wanted ads in local newspapers, professional association newsletters, and trade or professional journals:** Although this strategy has limited effectiveness (more than 80 percent of job openings are never advertised), you don't want to overlook the obvious.

2. **Contacting employment agencies and placement services:** The good news about employment agencies and placement services is that they do have job positions that they are trying to fill. But their services come with a possible buyer-beware sign. Make sure that you work with a firm that has a good reputation and that you understand the terms of their contract before you sign any agreement with them.

3. **Connecting with executive recruiters, who work the high end of the job market:** Stated differently, executive recruiters work with professionals and mid- to senior-level management executives who are interested in landing new jobs.

4. **Registering with database placement services/networks:** These services are relative newcomers to the employment market. They offer you the option to post your resume online or send it into a national service, and employers then pay to review your resume. While they have the advantage of convenience, they have the disadvantage of a tight job market where employers are less likely to pay to review applicant resumes.

5. **Joining professional associations:** Associations can have several potential benefits available to their job-hunting members, including membership directories (for networking purposes), networking meetings, and job banks or listings.

6. **Enlisting the assistance of career planning and placement services:** Students and alumni of many colleges and universities can avail themselves of job and career fairs, on-campus interviews, and alumni directories.

7. **Sending out targeted mailings to organizations and employers of interest in specific fields, industries, and geographic areas:** This strategy works most effectively when you target a specific person by name rather than relying on mass mailings or cold calls.

8. **Applying directly to employers:** You can find job openings through company Web sites or human resources offices.

9. **Developing a list of referrals through networking sources and conducting informational or exploratory interviews:** Informational interviews can help you learn more about the employer and its needs.

10. **Parlaying part-time, temporary, and contract positions into permanent full-time opportunities:** Companies sometimes use temp-to-hire and other such positions to employ workers on a trial basis. These positions are a good way to see if the company is a good fit for you as well.

11. **Employing yourself:** If you can't find the job of your dreams, you can work on creating that job for yourself through creative self-employment.

42. Help Wanted

*The gem cannot be polished without friction,
nor man perfected without trials.*

Chinese proverb

Sooner or later, almost every job hunter turns to the want ads hoping for an easy way to find the job of their dreams. Knowing how and when to use advertised listings is an important part of your job search.

1. Identify the newspapers, magazines, and trade publications that are most likely to advertise the kinds of positions that you are looking for.

2. Read the entire classified section from two or three past issues to get a feeling for how the information is organized.

3. Make a list of the job titles and section headings that are most appropriate for you and make sure that you check those job titles and section headings each and every time you read the ads.

4. Cut out or make copies of the ads that you want to respond to.

5. Review the ad carefully before responding. What qualifications are required? What are your greatest strengths and selling points? How do they prefer to receive responses? Remember to take your lead from their cues—if they say "No phone calls!", that means no phone calls.

6. If the ad requests that candidates send resumes, write a strong cover letter to send along with your resume. In your letter, stick as closely as you can to the language and information that is highlighted in the ad.

7. Make sure that you include an address, telephone number, and e-mail address where you can be reached.

8. If you haven't heard back from the employer after one week, follow up your letter and resume with a telephone call. In that conversation, confirm that your resume has been received, discuss your qualifications, and request an interview. FYI: Some employment experts estimate that follow-up phone calls increase the likelihood of getting an interview by 25 percent or more.

43. Is Anybody Home?

Motivation alone is not enough. If you have an idiot and you motivate him, now you have a motivated idiot.

Jim Rohn

Many people are used to being "plugged in" 24/7. But when you communicate with potential employers, you may want to think through your options carefully before deciding what numbers to give out on your resume and cover letters.

1. If you work a traditional 9-to-5 job, it may be most convenient for you to use your office phone number as your primary contact (assuming that your employer doesn't monitor your calls and that you'll have enough privacy to respond to a call from a prospective employer).

2. If it's too risky for you to use your office phone, cell phones are another option. If so, give some careful thought to how and when you normally use your cell phone, because you certainly don't want your seatmate on the train or the kid behind the Starbucks counter listening to your phone calls with prospective employers.

3. If you decide to use your home phone number as a primary contact, make sure that your phone message sounds professional rather than cute or overly friendly. (I'm still recovering from the woman who sang opera arias with her husband on their answering machine.)

4. If you share your home with other people (especially children), they will need to be instructed to answer the phone courteously and to always take messages.

5. E-mail offers another expedient way to communicate with employers. It is usually prudent, for the sake of privacy, to use your personal e-mail account rather than an office address.

6. Take the time to create a new e-mail address that reflects your professionalism. Potential employers don't need to know about the sexual preferences, drinking habits, or favorite hobbies that are often reflected in personal e-mail addresses.

44. Taking Advantage of Career Fairs

Cessation of work is not accompanied by cessation of expenses.

Cato the Elder

Career fairs are an excellent place to meet new employers and interview for possible jobs. But you need to do more than make 20 copies of your resume and have your business suit cleaned and pressed. You also need a game plan.

- ✔ Make sure that your resume is well-written and error-free. Generally speaking, you will want to print out copies (rather than use photocopies) because the quality will be better.

- ✔ Read the career fair handout in advance to figure out which companies will be represented. If possible, do some advance research on those companies so that you can present yourself intelligently.

- ✔ Focus on three to five companies that really interest you (rather than trying to cover the universe of employers). Try to engage the recruiters in an intelligent conversation about their company goals and priorities.

- ✔ Prepare a 30-second "elevator speech" to use with recruiters. Basically, this is a succinct introduction of who you are, what you know how to do, and why you are interested in them.

- ✔ When you give recruiters your resume, ask them what the next step in the process will be. Also, get their business card so that you can follow up with them if, for some reason, they neglect to follow up with you.

45. The Recruiter Connection

One of our greatest gifts is our intuition. It is a sixth sense we all have—we just need to learn to tap into and trust it.

Donna Karan

Executive recruiters can provide valuable job search assistance to professionals and executives, assuming you can find the right person for the job. Some of the things you need to know to make this relationship work:

1. Recruiters work for client companies rather than individuals, which means that you can't expect them to assume too much responsibility for your job search campaign. However, they do have access to bona fide job listings and are also rich in contacts, so it makes sense, whenever possible, to add a recruiter's name to your network of contacts.

2. Networking is usually the best way to get connected to a recruiter. Ask your friends and colleagues to recommend recruiters that they have worked with in the past. A recommendation from someone who is currently one of the recruiter's clients is akin to a magic bullet. It usually hits its mark early and often.

3. You can use *The Directory of Executive Recruiters* to identify recruiters who specialize in your field, industry, or job function. Rather than blanketing the recruiter marketplace with unsolicited resumes, selectively contact those people who work in your target market.

4. Some recruiters suggest that candidates telephone first before sending their resumes; other prefer to see your resume first before having any telephone discussions. Given the variation in their preferences, you'll probably need to work by trial and error to determine which approach is most effective for you.

5. Offer the recruiter a quid pro quo. Pass along information, refer them to potential client companies, and recommend other job hunters (who may be good candidates for different positions) in order to motivate the recruiter to want to help you in return.

6. Follow up resumes with telephone calls. If possible, try to get the recruiter to meet with you face-to-face as well. It's always better to be able to distinguish yourself with an in-person meeting.

7. Don't expect a recruiter to get you a job or get mad at them because haven't sent you out on enough interviews. They don't owe you a job, and because you haven't paid them a fee, you aren't entitled to any specific service. If they can help you, it's usually because they are working on an assignment for which you really are the best candidate. And if they don't help, more often than not it's because they don't think that you're the right candidate for the assignments that they are trying to fill. To them, it's not personal—it's just business.

46. Recruiter Worksheet

Everyone who got where he is has had to begin where he was.

Richard L. Evans

Name of recruiter: _____

Address: _____

Telephone number: _____

Fax number: _____

E-mail address: _____

Web site: _____

Method of contact: _____

Referral source: _____

Results: _____

_____

Follow-up: _____

47. Can an Employment Agency Help You?

Every great leap forward in your life comes after you have made a clear decision of some kind.

Brian Tracy

Finding an employment agency that is both reputable and useful to you in your job search requires some skill and persistence. Before you sign up for an agency's services, you need to ask some or all of the following questions:

- ✔ Does the agency specialize in any specific industry or area?
- ✔ What kinds of people do they prefer to work with?
- ✔ Who pays their fee?
- ✔ Does the job hunter need to sign an exclusive contract with them?
- ✔ Do they provide resume writing assistance?
- ✔ Do they coach candidates to be effective interviewees?
- ✔ Do they have job orders that match your qualifications and experience?

48. Employment Agency Worksheet

Name of agency: _____

Name of recruiter: _____

Address: _____

Phone number: _____

E-mail address: _____

Web site: _____

Areas of specialization: _____

Who pays the fee: _____

Services: _____

- Resume writing _____
- Interview coaching _____
- Placement _____

49. More Job Search Myths

Don't ask yourself what the world needs. Ask yourself what makes
you come alive, and then go and do that. Because what the
world needs is people who have come alive.

Howard Thurman

Myth #1:   The help-wanted ads are the best way to find a job.

False. Current statistics estimate that 60 percent of all new jobs are found through either networking or the Internet.

Myth #2:   A headhunter will find me a job.

Wrong again. Headhunters (or recruiters) work for the companies who pay them to find the best candidates for a job. While a headhunter may help you find a job, recruiters will always tell you that they work for the client companies who pay their fees.

Myth #3:   The best place to send resumes is the human resources department.

Also wrong. Human resources departments are usually in the business of screening out candidates or collecting resumes to pass along to the hiring manager. The best way to make contact with a potential employer is to go directly to the hiring manager whenever possible.

Myth #4:   It's who you know that matters most.

Yes and no. While it is true that many jobs are filled through word of mouth and referrals, what you know still matters as well. You can have the greatest connections in the world, but if you don't have the skills to back you up, you could still end up on the wrong side of the employment equation.

Myth #5:   There are no good jobs for people over 50.

Wrong, wrong, wrong. Without denying the reality of age discrimination in the workplace, it's important to realize that there are many people over 50 who are still able to land great new jobs. Before you leap to the ageism conclusion, make sure that you have really honed your marketable skills and can sell potential employers on your qualifications and experience.

Myth #6: You'll never get a good job without a college degree.

Also false. While it definitely helps to have a college pedigree to your name, it's your job to persuade employers that your practical experience makes you the most valuable candidate. Before you talk yourself into despair over your lack of an education, make sure that you are doing your part to convince employers that you have the smarts and skills to do the work they need done.

Myth #7: The more resumes you send out, the more likely it is that you will be successful in your job search.

Extremely doubtful. Most research indicates that targeted mailings are more effective than mass mailings when it comes to generating job leads and offers. By taking the time to do some quality research, target employers who can really use your experience, and generate good referrals, you are more likely to advance your job search cause in all of the right ways.

50. Networking Strategies for Success

Here are step-by-step instructions on using networking as a strategy in your job search.

1. **Get your goal in focus.** Decide what you want to do and where you want to do it. Use earlier checklists to identify key skills and potential employers.

2. **Prepare a contact list.** Include anyone who might have some information about your field. Think broadly.

3. **Contact your connections.** Meet with them to explain your goals, share your resume, and ask for advice and for referrals to others who might be able to help.

4. **Follow up.** Pursue any information, other contacts, and potential opportunities you learn about from your contacts. Make sure that you keep in touch with them by following up on leads and checking in for new information.

5. **Say thank you.** Be sure to formally thank all the people with whom you meet. Reciprocate by sharing information they might find useful.

6. **Attend programs and events.** Participate in all networking programs and services available through professional trade associations, alumni groups, and other membership organizations.

51. Network in Action

People who need people are the luckiest people in the world.

Bob Merrill

Use these pages to record your list of networking contacts. Then make a goal to add to the list on a daily basis.

EMPLOYMENT

Current employer:

Name: _____

Address: _____

Phone number: _____

Position: _____

E-mail address: _____

Relationship: _____

Date and method of contact: _____

What you discussed: _____

_____

Follow-up: _____

Former employers:

Name: _____

Address: _____

Phone number: _____

Position: _____

E-mail address: _____

Relationship: _____

Date and method of contact: _____

What you discussed: _____

_____

Follow-up: _____

Clients/customers

Name: _____

Address: _____

Phone number: _____

Position: _____

E-mail address: _____

Relationship: _____

Date and method of contact: _____

What you discussed: _____

_____

Follow-up: _____

Vendors

Name: _____

Address: _____

Phone number: _____

Position: _____

E-mail address: _____

(continued)

(continued)

Relationship: _____

Date and method of contact: _____

What you discussed: _____

_____

Follow-up: _____

Colleagues

Name: _____

Address: _____

Phone number: _____

Position: _____

E-mail address: _____

Relationship: _____

Date and method of contact: _____

What you discussed: _____

_____

Follow-up: _____

SCHOOL

Faculty

Name: _____

Address: _____

Phone number: _____

Position: _____

E-mail address: _____

Relationship: _____

Date and method of contact: _____

What you discussed: _____

_____

Follow-up: _____

Classmates

Name: _____

Address: _____

Phone number: _____

Position: _____

E-mail address: _____

Relationship: _____

Date and method of contact: _____

What you discussed: _____

_____

Follow-up: _____

Administration

Name: _____

Address: _____

Phone number: _____

Position: _____

E-mail address: _____

Relationship: _____

Date and method of contact: _____

(continued)

(continued)

What you discussed: _____

_____

Follow-up: _____

SOCIAL CONTACTS

Family

Name: _____

Address: _____

Phone number: _____

Position: _____

E-mail address: _____

Relationship: _____

Date and method of contact: _____

What you discussed: _____

_____

Follow-up: _____

Friends

Name: _____

Address: _____

Phone number: _____

Position: _____

E-mail address: _____

Relationship: _____

Date and method of contact: _____

What you discussed: _____

_____

Follow-up: _____

Neighbors

Name: _____

Address: _____

Phone number: _____

Position: _____

E-mail address: _____

Relationship: _____

Date and method of contact: _____

What you discussed: _____

_____

Follow-up: _____

Community or professional activities

Name: _____

Address: _____

Phone number: _____

Position: _____

E-mail address: _____

Relationship: _____

Date and method of contact: _____

What you discussed: _____

_____

(continued)

(continued)

Follow-up: _____

Clubs and social organizations

Name: _____

Address: _____

Phone number: _____

Position: _____

E-mail address: _____

Relationship: _____

Date and method of contact: _____

What you discussed: _____

_____

Follow-up: _____

Service people (attorneys, bankers, doctors, hairstylists)

Name: _____

Address: _____

Phone number: _____

Position: _____

E-mail address: _____

Relationship: _____

Date and method of contact: _____

What you discussed: _____

_____

Follow-up: _____

Other job hunters

Name: _____

Address: _____

Phone number: _____

Position: _____

E-mail address: _____

Relationship: _____

Date and method of contact: _____

What you discussed: _____

_____

Follow-up: _____

Others

Name: _____

Address: _____

Phone number: _____

Position: _____

E-mail address: _____

Relationship: _____

Date and method of contact: _____

What you discussed: _____

_____

Follow-up: _____

52. Eight Ways to Manage the Reference Process

Learning how to use your references properly is an important aspect of the entire job search process. The following checklist will help get you thinking in the right direction.

1. Never provide the names, addresses, and telephone numbers of your references on your resume or employment applications. You always want to meet with prospective employers first before providing them with any reference information.

2. Do not bring a list of your references with you to job interviews and offer them to the interviewer at the conclusion of an interview. After you interview for a position that interests you, you need to give careful thought to the best person to offer as a reference.

3. Try not to lose track of former employers, supervisors, and colleagues. If you have lost touch with some people, you may want to track them down early in your job search process so that you can reconnect with them to jog their memories about you, reestablish a connection, and give accurate reference information. If you haven't worked with your contact person in a while, give them a current copy of your resume and an overview of your current career goals.

4. Be creative about your reference choices. While direct supervisors are often useful choices (assuming, of course, that you had a good relationship with that person), other people can speak to different dimensions of your performance, including clients/customers, suppliers/vendors, co-workers, and even subordinates.

5. After you have interviewed for a position that interests you, contact your references again to ask permission to provide them as a contact person and give them an update on the position and the company that will be calling them. This information will allow your references to tailor their comments. Also, be sure to verify contact information, including telephone number, e-mail address, and best contact times.

6. When preparing your list of references for potential employers, provide some background details as to how you know each reference and the information they can confirm, as well as their name, telephone number, e-mail and physical addresses, and job title.

7. Reference lists are professional documents. They should always be typed and professionally formatted, preferably in a font and style that is consistent with your resume. If you send this information via e-mail, send it as an attachment so that it will look more professional.

8. After you have received and accepted a job offer, send each of your references a thank-you card to tell them about your success and express your appreciation to them for their help.

53. Job Search Insanity

Insanity: doing the same thing over and over again
and expecting different results.

Albert Einstein (attributed)

It's both easy and understandable to want to blame the job market for an extended bout of unemployment, but you do yourself a disservice if you aren't also willing to consider that you are contributing to your dilemma. It's easy to get frustrated with job hunting and conduct your search in a stale, half-hearted manner. If you continue to do what you've always done—network the same way, send out the same resume and cover letter, and use the same group of contacts over and over again—without much success, it may be time to change your approach.

To evaluate what you need to change, answer the following questions:

1. Which of your job search methods no longer seem to be working?

   ✔ Does your resume generate the kind of response you want?

   ✔ Do recruiters express interest in you and send you out to interview with prospective employers?

   ✔ Do the people in your network continue to send you leads, or do you have the sense that they're avoiding you or don't know how to help?

   ✔ Do the Web sites that you visit yield appropriate listings, or do you get the feeling that they don't have the kind of position you're looking for?

   As you approach the new work week, make a habit of reviewing this information and make whatever changes are necessary to generate new leads, motivation, and enthusiasm.

2. Which job search strategies and techniques are working to your satisfaction?

   Obviously, you don't need to fix what isn't broken—you just need to do more of what is working. When you get the kind of responses and feedback that you're looking for, it empowers you to get and stay motivated and optimistic.

3. Is there something new that you haven't yet tried?

   ✔ A new Web site?

   ✔ An electronic mailing list?

   ✔ A job club?

   ✔ A career counselor?

   Instead of dismissing these novelty approaches a priori, why not give them a chance to work for you? After all, you never know where your next job may come from.

54. Do You Need a Career Counselor?

The secret of greatness is simple: Do better work than any other man in your field—and keep on doing it.

Wilfred Peterson

A career counselor is a job search coach who can help you develop a career plan and implement a job search strategy. If any of the following situations apply to you, you might want to consider working with a career counselor.

1. I often get stuck in stressful and/or dead end jobs.

2. I don't know what I want to be when I grow up.

3. I have trouble getting along with my bosses or co-workers.

4. I often get passed over for promotions.

5. My work bores me.

6. I don't respect the people that I work for and with.

7. I feel like I'm not living up to my potential.

8. My work is meaningless.

9. I change jobs a lot, but the new job isn't any better than the last one.

10. I have trouble setting or meeting goals.

11. I had bigger dreams for myself.

12. I often get fired or laid off.

13. I have a reputation as a troublemaker.

14. People take advantage of me at work.

15. I never get any credit for the work that I do.

16. I feel like I don't have any skills.

17. It's hard to get up and go to work in the morning.

18. I don't know how to sell myself.

19. I feel like I don't have anything to offer an employer.

20. I never get the salary that I deserve.

21. My resume is a disaster.

22. I don't know what I want to do.

23. I don't know how to look for a job.

24. I hate authority.

25. I can't stand the people I work with.

26. I feel like an impostor at work.

27. I'm too much of a perfectionist.

28. My work doesn't fit my personality.

55. What Career Counselors Do

*If a man does not keep pace with his companions, perhaps
it is because he hears a different drummer. Let him step to the
music which he hears, however measured or far away.*

Henry David Thoreau

Here is a list of services career counselors offer.

1. Provide individual counseling for career choice, career development, and job search concerns.

2. Conduct career workshops and job support groups.

3. Administer and interpret vocational tests.

4. Teach job hunting skills and strategies.

5. Write resumes and cover letters.

6. Provide support during transitions.

7. Help resolve emotional and psychological conflicts.

8. Aid clients in developing career plans.

9. Refer clients to outside resources.

10. Help clients improve career decision-making and interpersonal skills.

11. Coordinate services with other helping professionals (social workers, psychiatrists, psychologists, and so on).

56. Finding the Right Counselor for You

I would rather have a mind opened by wonder than one closed by belief.

Gerry Spence, *How to Argue and Win Every Time*

If you decide to explore the possibility of working with a career counselor, it is important to choose someone whose style and values are compatible with your needs. There are a number of ways to identify good counselors.

1. Networking is usually one of the best methods. Talk to the people you know (including the career services office at your school or alma mater) about any career counselors who they know to be competent and reputable.

2. Use the telephone and Internet Yellow Pages to identify career counselors in your community.

3. When you have a name (or preferably a few names) of career counselors, call the counselors and interview them on the phone about their services.

4. Ask about credentials. Although career counselors do not have to be licensed in most states, it is in your best interest to inquire if a counselor has an advanced degree in psychology or counseling as well as specific training and experience in career and employment issues.

5. If you prefer to work with a counselor who is licensed or certified, you can find a list of those career counselors at the Web site of the National Board of Counselor Certification (www.nbcc.org). Use their CounselorFind feature to search for certified counselors by specialty and geographic location.

6. Ask about areas of specialization and experience. Some counselors either specialize in working with specific populations (for example, lawyers, doctors, or business executives) or have extensive experience with certain industries or occupations. Depending on your needs and situation, you may want to choose someone who is knowledgeable in your particular field or profession.

7. Counselors vary in regard to their use of testing instruments. If you are interested in testing, make sure that you choose someone who is comfortable and knowledgeable about these instruments and vice versa. You certainly wouldn't want to choose a counselor who relies heavily on testing if you prefer a counseling modality. Having said that, keep in mind that there are many counselors who provide both testing and counseling, depending on the specific needs of the client.

8. Some career counselors make a clear distinction between career counseling and personal counseling. Others, particularly those who are trained in psychology, recognize that feelings and conflicts may surface during a job search or career transition (fear of success, fear of failure, lack of support, and so on) and will work with you to help resolve those issues. If you sense that you might want to delve a little deeper, make sure that you choose a counselor who works psychologically.

9. Ask the counselor to provide you with the names and numbers of people they have worked with who can attest to their capabilities. Although some counselors may not be able to provide the names of former clients (for confidentiality purposes), they can and should refer you to professional colleagues who can attest to their capabilities.

57. Long-Distance Job Hunting

To me, it seems a dreadful indignity to have a soul controlled by geography.

George Santayana

Long-distance job hunting poses a unique set of challenges and therefore deserves special consideration.

1. Employers prefer to hire familiar faces. Although you know that you are not a visitor from outer space—just another city or state—you may be perceived as an alien from another planet. To overcome this perceptual barrier, you will need to familiarize yourself with the city's landscape and resources.

2. If you already have contacts in your target location, recruit them as allies in your job search. Ask them to send you a copy of the local telephone directory and provide you with the names of major newspapers, business directories, or locale-specific job search books.

3. Don't worry if you don't have contacts in your target location; you can gather this information yourself by contacting the local Chamber of Commerce to obtain business directories and any other available information.

4. If you currently live in a city with a good library, the business librarian (or any librarian who is familiar with the library's job search and business resources) can help you identify and locate the information that you need.

5. Plan to subscribe to the local newspapers. Many newspapers now have online editions, which make it easier to access local information and job listings in a timely manner.

6. Join a professional association with a national membership and then obtain the names of the people who head the chapters in your target areas. Network with these people by telephone or e-mail to make new contacts and learn more about the city's resources.

7. You can also use the professional organization's membership directory to conduct informational interviews by telephone. Also, don't overlook the many potential contacts available through alumni directories from your alma mater. These directories have proved invaluable to many job hunters who are looking to relocate.

8. When you have the names of potential contacts, decide on your preferred method of contact. If you represent yourself well on the phone, you can warm up the conversation with small talk. If you prefer to write first (and call later), e-mail usually works best, as it is quicker and more efficient than traditional snail mail.

9. Never send your resume to a new contact person as an attachment because they will probably be afraid to open it. In general, it makes more sense to build some of your resume information into the content of your e-mail and send the resume at a later date after you have established a contact.

10. Depending on your profession and level of experience, you can also benefit from contacting executive recruiters who specialize in your target location. If necessary, revisit the information in Checklist 45 for ideas about how to make this strategy work for you.

11. Plan to visit the city, preferably around industry conferences and trade shows, so that you can make as many contacts as possible in the shortest amount of time. Also, take the initiative to set up informational or exploratory interviews while you are in the city in order to become a familiar face.

12. Stay in touch with your contacts. When you are far away, it is a little too easy for them to forget you. It's your job to make sure that you become memorable and keep them motivated on your behalf.

58. Working Globally

A man's homeland is wherever he prospers.

Aristophanes

The world is a complicated place, and if you think that job searching within the United States is tough, it's even more confusing when you want to live and work abroad. Fortunately, there are lots of resources that you can use to get the so-called "lay of the land."

✔ Going Global (www.going-global.com) is a Web site designed primarily to meet the needs of international job seekers and professionals. It contains a comprehensive array of country-specific career information, including resume/CV writing advice, job sources, interviewing strategies, salary negotiations, and work permit and visa regulations. It also has country guides, which you can purchase for a reasonable fee; they are well worth the investment.

✔ Expat Exchange (www.expatexchange.com) is a virtual community that connects people who are relocating to, living in, or returning from more than 135 overseas locations. This site provides a great way to network with people who have "been there and done that," as well as experts and regional contacts who can answer more specific questions.

✔ The International Jobs Center (www.internationaljobs.org) is a membership organization that provides extensive information on international jobs. This includes a weekly newspaper with more than 500 job postings, profiles of major employers in the international development market, and an e-mail notification system to alert you to new job openings in your areas of interest.

✔ Overseasjobs.com (www.overseasjobs.com) is part of the Aboutjobs.com network of sites (www.aboutjobs.com) that provide free services to job seekers (employers must pay to list positions). The site has lots of useful information, including country guides, informative articles, visa/work permit information, and job listings.

59. Managing Your Finances During a Job Search

I am having an out-of-money experience.

Author unknown

The financial challenge of managing unemployment is often scary. But it's important to separate your disaster fantasies from the reality of your situation and act accordingly.

1. Are you eligible for unemployment? If so, figure the amount here. _____

2. Have you talked to your employer about severance pay (which is often part of a termination package)? If not, what's stopping you? If so, how much? _____

3. Are you vested in a pension or profit-sharing plan? Do you know the numbers and details of those accounts? _____

4. Do you have a 401(k) with your employer? Do you have all of the information you need about that account? _____

5. Is your employer offering you outplacement assistance to help you find new work? If you can negotiate this benefit, it can save you lots of time and money by providing you with resume writing, job counseling, and (in some cases) a place to go every day where you can conduct your job search in the context of community. _____

6. What about insurance benefits? Are you eligible for COBRA? Do you know how much the premiums will cost? Have you looked into other (less-expensive) insurance options? _____

7. Do you need to supplement your family income with part-time, temporary, or contract work? If so, do you know how to get started? Or how to figure out how to get started? _____

8. Have you calculated your fixed expenses?

Rent/mortgage: _____

Utilities: _____

Telephone: _____

Automobile: _____

Insurance: _____

Loans: _____

Food: _____

Clothing: _____

Education: _____

Household expenses: _____

Miscellaneous: _____

Total: _____

9. How long can you realistically afford to be unemployed? _____

10. Can you borrow money if you need it? If so, from whom? _____

11. If you need more time, can you think of other ways to earn extra money (e.g. hobbies, skills, small business activities)? List them here:

_____

_____

_____

60. Time Management for Job Hunters

An unhurried sense of time is in itself a form of wealth.

Bonnie Friedman

It's often been said that finding a job is a full-time job. This advice is fine if you're unemployed, but it is less useful if you already have a full-time job that requires your attention. To get better control over your job search time, follow the guidelines below:

1. Set reasonable job search goals—either by time spent or activity accomplished. If you have a limited amount of time to conduct your job search, strive for efficiency and set your goals by activity rather than the clock. This kind of structure will give you a greater sense of accomplishment.

2. Chunk your activities together for maximum efficiency. For example, set aside blocks of time exclusively for Internet research, make several phone calls sequentially, or write your resume. This method will enable you to focus and concentrate exclusively on the task at hand rather than trying to squeeze too many different activities into too little space. Make sure to set achievable goals in each category.

3. Create a place to keep track of your job search activities. You can use a simple spreadsheet or word-processor document or make a chart in a notebook to list your activities along with the time you spent on them, the people you've contacted, the results, follow-up tasks you need to complete, and any other relevant information. Having such a file will help you quickly locate information you need when an employer or other contact calls.

4. Reward yourself when you have completed your job search tasks competently and effectively by doing something you really enjoy.

5. When time is limited, procrastination is not an option. Don't let yourself be sidelined with unimportant activities. If you can't make your job search one of your priorities, you can't realistically expect to find a good job.

6. Carve out a physical space for yourself that enables you to have some expectation of privacy. The kitchen table is not a place for quality solitude or communication with potential contacts and employers.

7. Learn to view each obstacle as a challenge to your problem-solving skills. After all, if finding a new job were easy, you would have done it weeks or months or years ago.

8. For those of you who have the opposite problem—meaning that you are unemployed and have too much time on your hands—you need to approach your situation differently. Most importantly, do not conduct your job search in total isolation. If you have access to outplacement services or a transition center, make it a point to go to their offices several times a week because people often find it easier to conduct a job search when everyone around them is engaged in the same activity.

9. Make sure that your job search includes plenty of networking time as well as both social and professional activities. If possible, join a professional group or weekly job club and participate in their events. Even if you aren't a particularly social person, try to force yourself to stay socially motivated. Successful job hunting is often a very social experience—so socialize!

10. Don't get distracted by household tasks or chores. If you're at home during the day, don't think that you don't have anything to do. For you, looking for a job really is a full-time job.

11. Don't neglect your physical or mental health. Job hunting is stressful, and you need to develop your own personal stress-busting strategies in the form of exercise, meditation, gardening, or whatever works for you.

61. Job Search Checklist

*Always bear in mind that your own resolution to succeed
is more important than any other one thing.*

Abraham Lincoln

1. Do you check several job posting sites (such as Monster.com [www.monster.com] or Careerbuilder.com [www.careerbuilder.com]) every day and submit your resume to appropriate positions?

2. Do you subscribe to at least one trade journal or professional publication with job listings?

3. Are you member of at least one professional association in your industry?

4. Do you have a membership directory for a professional trade group, networking group, or alumni association that you can use for networking purposes?

5. Have you reviewed your resume to make sure that it is on target and error free?

6. Are you doing Internet research to identify companies that might be interested in hiring you?

7. Do you have an actionable networking strategy?

8. Are you conducting informational or exploratory interviews as part of your networking strategy?

9. Are you persistent in following up on all job leads?

10. Have you researched and contacted employment agencies or executive recruiters in your industry or occupation?

11. Do you know how to interview, or do you need more interviewing preparation and practice?

12. Have you contacted your references to ask permission to use their names?

13. Do you know how to communicate your strengths and weaknesses and target employers who can benefit from your qualifications and experience?

14. Do you have family and friends who can support you through this process?

15. Have you determined whether you can benefit from a career counselor and identified and contacted career counselors who can coach you on job search strategies and techniques?

62. Secrets of a Successful Job Search

They always say time changes things,
but you actually have to change them yourself.

Andy Warhol

To conduct a successful job search, you need to manage both the logistical dimensions and your own attitudes and feelings. A summary of what (I hope) you now realize that it takes to succeed:

1. You have established your job search goals and objectives.

2. You can articulate what you are looking for.

3. You can discuss your strengths and qualifications with networking contacts and potential employers.

4. You know how to research your job targets and identify job leads.

5. You feel positive about your job search direction and strategy.

6. You have a network of people you can contact or, in the alternative, a strategy to develop new contacts and resources.

7. You have—or can develop—a support system for yourself during your transition.

8. You are willing to work hard to find a new job.

9. You have the ability and desire to learn from your mistakes.

10. You are able to manage your negative feelings and thoughts.

11. You can recognize when you need help and aren't afraid to ask for assistance and guidance.

12. You are able to motivate yourself and take responsibility for your actions.

The Interview

Interviewing requires a "practice makes perfect" mentality. This section shows you how to develop successful interviewing strategies and techniques.

63. Interviewing: What Employers Look For

The newest computer can merely compound, at speed, the oldest problem in the relations between human beings, and in the end the communicator will be confronted with the old problem, of what to say and how to say it.

Edward R. Murrow

Every year, hundreds of millions of dollars are wasted because candidates are hired for positions they aren't qualified for, while others are turned down for jobs that they are more qualified to fill. To make sure that you don't become one of these workplace casualties, you need to take the time to understand what employers are looking for.

1. Shared values

   Companies often espouse a particular set of values and ideals. Review their mission statement to determine what those values and ideals are.

2. Commitment

   Most employers are fearful of job hoppers. Although it's no longer expected that employees will spend their entire careers in one place, employers do want to know that you are going to do more than collect a paycheck and use them as a stepping stone in your career ladder.

3. Energy and enthusiasm

   Employers are impressed with candidates who have the desire, enthusiasm, and energy to do the work they are hired to do—and more.

4. An innovative spirit

   Many employers are seeking to gain the competitive edge and, in that spirit, are seldom content with the status quo. Translation: They look for employees who bring a sense of creativity and innovation to their jobs.

5. Responsiveness

   Employers want their people to be responsive to their organizational goals and needs. It's good to be able to work independently, but it's also important to acknowledge and be comfortable with the reality that you work for them.

6. Accountability

   The buck has to stop somewhere and there are times when it will stop with you as the responsible employee. This means that you must be willing to take responsibility for your mistakes and be willing to be accountable to the people you work for and with.

7. Team players

   Many employers want team players who can work collaboratively more than they want individual stars. In a technologically advanced, highly competitive workplace, they look to hire people who can work together effectively.

8. Compatibility

   Managers prefer to hire employees who will improve their own standing in the organization. Demonstrate that you can look good and they'll race to hire you for their team.

9. Communication skills

   The ability to communicate—both verbally and in writing—is an essential skill set in every industry and profession.

10. Style

    Employers also evaluate how an individual's work style fits in with their organizational culture. If there's a match, this can be an important factor in the hiring process.

64. The Art and Skill of Preparation

For good or ill, your conversation is your advertisement. Every time you open your mouth you let men look into your mind. Do they see it well clothed, neat, businesswise?

Bruce Burton

When it comes to job interviewing, winging it is not an option. To find—and get—the best position, you must prepare often and well.

- ✔ Determine your marketable skills. These include technical qualifications, general liberal-arts skills (analytical, communication, problem solving), and character traits (honesty, trustworthiness, dependability)
- ✔ Develop a selling strategy to persuade employers that you have the right stuff to do the job.
- ✔ Learn to tell stories. Review your work experience and be prepared to give examples that demonstrate your skills and qualifications.
- ✔ Anticipate tough questions. For better or worse, employers can be cynical and suspicious that candidates are trying to fool them with lies and half-truths. Recognizing the potential stumbling blocks in your history will enable you to anticipate and strategize effective ways of overcoming these obstacles.
- ✔ Research the company/organization. To understand the needs and values of potential employers, tap into your own network and go online to find out whatever you can about the company and the kind of person they are most likely to be looking for.
- ✔ Deal with sensitive information sensitively. After you gain insight into an organization's challenges and liabilities, you need to deal with that information tactfully. Like individuals, organizations have emotional sore spots that, if pointed out in the wrong way, can make people defensive.
- ✔ Organize. As part of your interview preparation, you will also need to handle logistical matters. By managing issues of time and place well, you create an impression of competence and professionalism.

✔ Negotiate. As you and your future employer explore the question of "fit," you may be asked to discuss compensation. Although it's best to postpone salary discussions until you have an offer, you must be prepared to handle the question whenever it surfaces in the process.

✔ Practice makes perfect. Great interviewing skills are not learned overnight. To be effective in job interviews, you need to develop a practice-and-perfection mentality. This means learning from your mistakes, revisiting your communications strategy, and improving your responses.

65. Body English

Your business clothes are naturally attracted to staining liquids.
This attraction is strongest just before an important meeting.

Scott Adams

You never get a second chance to make a first impression, which means that you have to do everything in your power to make that first impression a good one.

1. Dress for success. An interview is a formal employment occasion. Treat it accordingly and wear your best suit or dress.

2. Your handshake is as important as your resume. It has to be strong, confident, and assertive.

3. Your energy level communicates interest and enthusiasm. Get plenty of sleep and make sure that you are alert and ready to engage the interviewer.

4. Posture also communicates energy. Sit up straight and look like you're alive, please.

5. A smile is worth a thousand words. It says "It's nice to meet you and I'm happy to be here."

66. Interview Do's and Don'ts

Knowledge is power.

Sir Francis Bacon

1. Do dress for respect—conservatively and professionally.

2. Don't sit passively in your seat and wait for the interviewer to do all of the work.

3. Do make small talk and try to find areas of common interest with interviewers, who are—believe it or not—people, too.

4. Don't look as if you are facing a firing squad. Smile and try to relax.

5. Do make sure to research the organization before the interview. This shows interviewers that you are genuinely interested in them.

6. Don't be late. This makes a terrible first impression. Instead, make sure that you have proper directions and leave plenty of time (in case traffic is bad, the bus is late, or you get lost).

7. Do bring extra copies of your resume in case the interviewer forgets or misplaces your original copy.

8. Don't call the interviewer by his or her first name unless they specifically instruct you to do so.

9. Do remember the interviewer's name and use it periodically throughout the interview.

10. Don't dominate the conversation. Your answers should always be succinct, direct, and well articulated.

11. Do learn to listen attentively and show genuine interest and enthusiasm. Remember, employers want people who care.

12. Don't deliver answers to interview questions as if you were making a speech. Although you should prepare responses to typical questions in advance, your delivery should sound sincere and unrehearsed. Remember: Make conversation, not presentations.

13. Do ask intelligent questions. Ask about job responsibilities, company goals, and other related topics.

14. Don't initiate conversations about money or benefits until you have a job offer. After you have received an offer, you have a lot more negotiating power.

15. Do present a confident self-image that offsets any concerns that you may be hiding something or have skeletons in your professional closet.

16. Don't lie or get defensive. Try to frame negative situations as positively as possible (in terms of a "mismatch," "different styles," or what you learned) without speaking badly about past employers or colleagues.

17. Do answer the questions fully and punctuate your answers with good stories that illustrate your competencies and style.

18. Don't beat yourself up for making mistakes. It's part of the process. The important thing is that you learn from those mistakes so that you don't repeat them in future interviews.

19. Do follow up. If you agreed to provide references or additional information, make sure that you deliver on your promises.

20. Don't forget to send a thank-you note either by e-mail or snail mail. In your letter, reassert your interest and qualifications.

21. Do continue to conduct your job search and look for additional opportunities. As Yogi Berra is famous for saying, "It ain't over till it's over."

22. Don't sit around waiting for the interviewer to call you. If you don't hear from them within a week after your interview, make sure that you check in to see where they (and you) are in the process.

23. Do remember that "no" doesn't always mean forever. Although you may not always get a job offer, if you stay on cordial terms with the people who interview you, you may end up hearing from them again.

24. Never burn bridges. However disappointed or rejected you may feel, try your best not to take it personally. Make sure that the interviewer knows that you enjoyed meeting them and are still interested in future possibilities.

25. Do move on. There are many, many fish in the sea of jobs—your challenge is to is to spot them and catch them.

67. Listening Skills 101

You can communicate best when you first listen.

Catherine Pulsifer

Communication is always a two-way street. In order to be responsive to interviewers' needs, you must know how to listen and listen well. To improve your listening skills:

1. Focus your attention on what the interviewer is saying. If your mind starts to wander, consciously force yourself to listen for the content, even if the interviewer's intonation is boring or the questions are phrased in a rambling manner.

2. Respond with appropriate nonverbal cues. Smile or nod your head in agreement when appropriate. Conversely, don't roll your eyes, clench your fists, or grimace at the interviewer's words.

3. Resist the impulse to interrupt.

4. Listen non-defensively. Do not be judgmental or critical of what you hear. This will only prevent you from truly understanding what the interviewer is saying.

5. Don't get distracted by trivial things that don't really matter, like the interviewer's appearance, accent, lisp, or lipsmacking. Respond to what is being said rather than how it is being communicated. Not everyone is a great communicator.

68. Expecting the Unexpected

A thing long expected takes the form of the unexpected when at last it comes.

Mark Twain

Nothing in life taxes your flexibility quite like interviewing. Here are some of the interviewing scenarios you might expect to encounter:

1. Screening interviews usually take place on the telephone and are conducted by a human resources professional or executive recruiter. Their goal is to determine whether you have the minimum qualifications to do the job and then move you along to the next person in the hiring hierarchy.

2. Sequential interviews take place in organizations that prefer to hire by consensus. As a result, you may find yourself meeting with several hiring authorities over the course of a day, a week, or a month. The key here is to approach each interview with freshness and enthusiasm. Don't worry about repeating yourself; this will only make you look consistent—not boring.

3. Group interviews can be conducted by a handful of people simultaneously or resemble a regular mob scene (with a cast of dozens). These interviews are usually more about presentation than conversation, but you should still try to establish rapport with each and every person in the room whenever possible. Candidates with group training or facilitation skills definitely have the edge in group interviews.

4. Stress interviews are another variety. While most interviews are by definition stressful, stress interviews are intentionally and artificially stressful. The intention of these interviews is mostly to see how you react to pressure and stress—the key is to recognize that you're in a stress interview and keep your cool!

5. Performance interviews often require that you give a presentation to an audience as a way of showcasing your platform skills and expertise. You will usually receive an assigned topic in advance, enabling you to prepare the information that you want to deliver in an organized and articulate manner.

6. Many employers like to supplement their interview process with aptitude, personality, and values tests. The experts vary in their advice about how to deal with these tests. My advice is to be truthful and to make sure that you always put the best spin on the truth. Answer questions with confidence, enthusiasm, and skill.

7. Computer-assisted interviews are changing the face of the selection process. During a computer-assisted interview, you will often be asked to sit at a computer terminal and enter information into the computer or answer by using a touch-tone phone. The thing to remember here is that you shouldn't say anything to a computer that you wouldn't say to an interviewer in a face-to-face meeting.

8. Mealtime interviews are a challenge for many reasons. Because of the more relaxed atmosphere, interviewers sometimes ask personal questions that would otherwise be considered illegal in a more formal setting. Don't be lulled into shooting yourself in the foot. Make sure you use your company manners and keep your game face on. You don't want to lose out on an interesting opportunity over the price of a steak dinner.

69. "Food, Glorious Food" and Other Challenges of Mealtime Interviews

Never eat more than you can lift.

Miss Piggy

Mealtime interviews pose a unique set of interviewing challenges, which are outlined below:

1. Keep drinking to a minimum, or better yet, don't drink at all.

2. Don't order anything messy. It's hard to concentrate on the interview when your spaghetti is dribbling down your chin.

3. No smoking, please—even if you're sitting in the smoking section of the restaurant.

4. Keep it simple. Never order too much food or choose the most expensive item on the menu. It's not your last meal and, as you've probably heard, there's no such thing as a free lunch.

5. Remember your company manners. No matter how comfortable you feel during the interview, don't shovel your food into your mouth, talk with your mouth full, or eat with your hands (unless it's finger food).

6. Keep the conversation friendly but professional. While you want to be likeable and charming, you don't want to turn on the conversational faucet by sharing too much personal information.

70. Typical Questions

Mend your speech a little, lest it may mar your fortunes.
William Shakespeare

Use this list of common interview questions to prepare ahead of time. Although you don't want to sound like you're reciting a canned answer, keeping some key points in mind can be helpful.

1. Tell me about yourself.
2. Why did you leave your last job?
3. What are your strengths?
4. What are your weaknesses?
5. Why should I hire you?
6. What are your career goals and objectives?
7. How does this job fit into your career goals?
8. What do you know about our organization?
9. How do you normally handle change?
10. What would you last employer say about you?
11. If you could do anything in your career differently, what would it be?
12. Describe your greatest achievement.
13. Describe your most significant failure.
14. Which of your jobs did you like the best? Why?
15. Which of your jobs did you like the least? Why?
16. What kind of employee are you?
17. How do you handle authority?
18. On your last performance evaluation, what did your manager criticize you for?

19. How do you handle conflict with peers?

20. How do you normally handle criticism?

21. Describe your relationship with your last manager.

22. Where do you want to be five years from now?

23. Why do you want to work for us?

24. Why have you changed jobs so often?

25. Why is it taking you so long to find a job?

26. Tell me about a time when you handle to handle a crisis situation.

27. How do you deal with stress and pressure?

28. How much are you presently earning?

29. How much money do you want?

30. When can you start?

31. Can we check your references?

32. Where else are you interviewing?

33. Is there anything that we have forgotten to ask you?

34. Do you have any questions for us?

71. "Tell Me About Yourself."

Not that the story need be long,
but it will take a long while to make it short.

Henry David Thoreau

"Tell me about yourself." This is one of the questions that strikes dread in the heart of many job hunters. But there's really no reason to panic because it's a golden opportunity for you to shine. To make your answer stand out from the competition, here are a few things that you might want to keep uppermost in your mind.

1. Interviewers do not want to hear your entire life story. What they do want to see and hear is how you present yourself, what you choose to focus on, and how you organize that information.

2. Always script out and rehearse your response before delivering it, but when you deliver your message, relax and make it interesting. Nobody wants to listen to a canned speech.

3. Time yourself to make sure that your spiel is no longer than two to three minutes. After that, interviewers tend to get bored and stop paying attention.

4. Focus on those aspects of your experience, education, and skill set that are most relevant to the open position. Don't focus on skills and experience that are unrelated to the company's needs; this will only emphasize that you are the wrong candidate for the job.

5. End the question with a question. For example, ask them if there is some component of your experience that they would like to hear about in greater detail or put the ball back in the court by asking them to tell you more about the position and the organization.

72. "Where Do You Want to Be Five Years from Now?"

The future ain't what it used to be.

Yogi Berra

This is another one of those typical questions that job hunters hate. Given the turbulent state of the economy and the job market, who can predict where they are going to be next week or next month or next year—let alone five years from now? Actually, you can—or at least you can try.

Strategies for dealing with this question:

1. Name a specific career goal: "My career goal is to become a _____."

2. Describe a flexible career goal: "Depending on your organizational goals and needs, I can see myself moving in several different ways. For example, _____."

3. Answer the question with a question: "What do you see this position leading to in the future?"

4. Find out where the last person who held the job went. (Hopefully, it was up and not out.)

5. Explain your needs and desire for growth and advancement without naming a specific path or paths.

73. The 25 Most Popular Behavioral Questions

Actions speak louder than words.

Proverb

Behavioral questions are based on the assumption that past performance is the best predictor of future success. Interviewers who rely on this style usually ask for specific information rather than asking general, open-ended questions and build those questions around the job descriptions. Here are some possible behavioral questions.

Tell me about a time when you

1. Worked effectively under pressure.
2. Handled a difficult situation with a co-worker.
3. Used your creativity to solve a problem.
4. Missed an obvious solution to a problem.
5. Were unable to complete a project on time.
6. Persuaded team members to do things your way.
7. Anticipated and averted potential problems.
8. Wrote a report that was well-received.
9. Had to make an important decision with limited information.
10. Were forced to make an unpopular decision.
11. Had to adapt to a difficult situation.
12. Tolerated opinions that were different from your own.
13. Felt disappointed in your own behavior.
14. Used your people skills to get your own way.
15. Had to deal with an irate customer.
16. Delegated an assignment or project that succeeded.

17. Surmounted a difficult obstacle.

18. Set your sights too high or too low.

19. Prioritized a complex project.

20. Won or lost an important contract.

21. Had to fire someone for cause.

22. Made a bad decision.

23. Hired the wrong person.

24. Turned down a good job.

25. Were terminated from a job.

74. Strategies for Dealing with Behavioral Questions

God is in the details.

Le Corbusier

Behavioral questions pose a difficult challenge for interviewees who prefer to view the interview as a conversation with a purpose between equals because they undercut rapport and often take on a very aggressive note.

1. Don't be intimidated by the format. If you don't understand the question, make sure that you ask for clarification rather than trying to guess what the interviewer is looking for.

2. Although you may be understandably anxious when confronted with behavioral directives, don't sabotage yourself by telling stories that will hurt you. Any time you say negative things about yourself or anyone else, you introduce an element of hostility into the interview. By putting a positive spin on your answers, you do your part to keep the tone of the interview positive.

3. Use the P-A-R format when preparing your story examples:

   P(roblem) or Situation: Describe the problem or situation that you were facing.
   A(ction): Describe the action that you took to deal with the problem or situation.
   R(esults): Describe the results of your action.

4. After you tell your story in response to a behavioral directive, ask for feedback. Is this the kind of information that the interviewer was looking for? Or would they like you to give a different example?

5. Frame your responses to focus on those examples or experiences that seem to fit most closely with your understanding of the organization and the open position.

6. Don't be afraid to say "I don't know" or "Nothing comes to mind." Remember, you can't invent experiences (positive or negative) that you don't have.

75. The Consultative Selling Approach to Interviewing

When people talk, listen completely. Most people never listen.

Ernest Hemingway

People who sell professional services often use what is called "consultative selling" in order to develop customer-focused services and solutions. Because job hunting is a one-person sales and marketing campaign, many of the same strategies and techniques can be applied to job interviews.

1. Never sell yourself in a vacuum. Before you launch into your "sales pitch," make sure that you understand your "customer's" (interviewer's) needs and problems.

2. Jobs exist for a purpose—to fulfill some business need or solve some business problem. By asking good questions and listening carefully to the answers, you can understand what kinds of problems and challenges the person in the position will be asked to resolve.

3. When you know what those problems and challenges are, you can customize your responses to focus on the specific skills and experiences that are most relevant to the position.

4. Consultative sales calls are not hard sells; they are two-way conversations in which the candidate works hard to demonstrate how their product (themselves) is the ideal solution to the employer's problems.

5. Listen twice as much as you speak. This means both listening to what is being said and listening for what is not being said. If you can ferret out the reservations or concerns beneath the questions, you are in a better position to position yourself as the answer to the employer's business problem.

6. Tell stories that give specific examples and tangible evidence of your relevant accomplishments in order to help the employer visualize you in action.

7. After you answer the question you've been asked, take the initiative to follow up with a question of your own. Your questions can take one of several forms. For example, you can ask them if this is the kind of information they were looking for or if they would like you to elaborate. You can ask them a similar question: Can you describe your organizational culture? Can you tell me more about the person this position reports to?

8. Keep in mind that rapport matters as much as content. Most employers feel reassured when they know that a candidate understands their problems and is responsive to their needs.

76. Problem-Solving Questions

If nothing else, the brain is an educational toy.

Tom Robbins

Many employers now use problem-solving or case-analysis questions in an effort to discover how candidates really think and perform (rather than how they say they work). This format shifts the emphasis from finding the "right answer" to showing that you know how to figure out the correct answer.

1. While the interviewer describes the scenario or problem to be solved, listen intently to what you are being asked to do.

2. Ask clarifying questions to determine what the interviewer is looking for.

3. Describe how you would gather information and data necessary to make an informed decision.

4. Discuss how you would use that data and information to generate options.

5. Explain the criteria you would use to make your final decision.

Example: An experienced sales rep was handed a ballpoint pen and given the instruction "Sell me this pen."

Her strategy:

1. Clarify whether the employer has established an intended market and, if so, whom the company has identified as its target market.

2. Determine the pen's best features and how they are beneficial to this market.

3. Discuss different ways to conduct market research (focus groups, telemarketing surveys, and so on) to learn more about the market.

4. Discuss ways that the data could be used to develop effective selling strategies.

77. "What Are Your Weaknesses?"

Good people are good because they've come to wisdom through failure.

William Saroyan

"Why do they always ask this question?" one of my clients complained. "It's so lame."

The answer is simple. They ask it because many candidates tell them the naked unadorned truth about their worst traits and characteristics. To make sure you don't do so, decide in advance how you want to answer this particular question. Some possible strategies:

1. Present a potential strength as a weakness. "Sometimes I lose track of time and work too hard." "It's hard for me to send out anything that isn't perfect."

2. Cite a corrected weakness. "I didn't get a chance to do enough programming at my last job, so I enrolled in courses at the community college to make sure that I didn't fall behind."

3. Cite a learning goal. "I would like to become more fluent in Spanish."

4. Cite a lesson learned. "I used to be overly sensitive to criticism. But now I realize that constructive criticism is an essential form of feedback."

5. Cite an unrelated skill. "I never learned how to drive a stick shift."

6. Defer to a greater authority. "Ask my parole officer." (Okay, maybe not.)

7. Refuse to answer on the grounds that it may incriminate you. "I'm not aware of any weaknesses that would interfere with my ability to do this job."

78. Red Flags: Dealing with Employer Objections

The real art of conversation is not only to say the right thing in the right place, but far more difficult, to leave unsaid the wrong thing at the tempting moment.

Dorothy Nevill

Employers will often go to great lengths to expose your flaws. They will bait you with negative questions, interrogate you about your weaknesses, and invent challenges for you to master. Your goal is not to take the bait and to rise to the occasion in ways that help you allay their fears.

1. Face reality. No one is perfect—and that includes you. This means that you need to take a careful look at your history to determine your personal Achilles' heel.

2. Employment history is one area of potential contention. Because past history often predicts future performance, employers are understandably concerned about job-hopping, employment gaps, and unexplained terminations. Your goal is to put the best face on the truth by convincing employers that these perceived problems are not liabilities for them—in other words, they won't interfere with your performance or longevity with them.

3. If an employer is concerned about your qualifications or suspects that you don't have enough experience to do the job, your goal should be to illustrate the transferability of your skills, your desire to learn, and your enthusiasm for the work. Remember, if you had already done everything that the job required, they'd probably say that you were overqualified because there would be nothing left for you to learn.

4. If an employer thinks that you are overqualified, ask them to explain why they feel that way. Sometimes this is a euphemism for age discrimination, concerns that you will be too expensive, or worries that you will get bored and leave. When you know what their real concerns are, you are in a better position to address their reservations.

5. If an employer expresses concern that you don't have a college degree, you need to question why they feel that this position requires a degree and if there is something in your experience or skill set that is deficient. If there is something that they would like you to learn at school, offer to take the courses that they feel are important *after* they hire you.

79. Overcoming Objections

Communication sometimes is not what you first hear.
Listen not just to the words, but listen for the reason.
Catherine Pulsifer

Interviewers' objections are a call to action. Whenever you encounter resistance from employers, your goal is to neutralize—and then overcome—their objections.

1. **Rephrase.** Start by summarizing your understanding of their concerns in your own words. (For example, you might say, "You seem concerned that I might not stay in this job for more than six months.")

2. **Confirm.** Check with the employer to determine whether your perception is accurate. (For example, "Do I understand you correctly?")

3. **Acknowledge.** Concede the concern, but not the liability. (For example, "I can understand why you might think that.")

4. **Neutralize.** Provide new information or redirect the conversation toward a more positive anchor. (For example, "To be honest with you, I'm excited about the potential in this job and would love to be able to build a long-term career at this company.")

5. **Recount.** Tell a story or mention an accomplishment that will help alleviate the interviewer's anxiety. (For example, "During the four years that I spent at _____, I was never bored or restless because there were always new challenges and opportunities for growth.")

80. Know Your Rights

*Remember this—that there is a proper dignity and proportion
to be observed in the performance of every act of life.*

Marcus Aurelius

Title VII of the Civil Rights Act of 1964 forbids employers from discriminating against any person on the basis of sex, race, age, national origin, or religion.

Title 1 of the Americans with Disabilities Act (1991) protects people with disabilities from discrimination in any aspect of employment, including application procedures, hiring, training, compensation, fringe benefits, or promotion.

The Age Discrimination Employment Act (1967) prohibits discrimination in employment against workers age 40 or older and promotes employment of older workers.

It's very hard to prove that an employer has discriminated against you. Even when an employer asks an illegal question, it may come down to your word against theirs if there aren't any witnesses to the conversation. If you feel that a potential employer has been particularly insulting, you do have the option to consult with an employment attorney. You also have the option to confront the employer (but don't expect them to hire you after a confrontation). If you think that the employer is actually ignorant about the illegality of their actions, you can try to educate them about more appropriate hiring practices.

81. Handling Illegal Questions

What corrupts communication? Anger, fear, prejudice, egotism, and envy.

Guy de Maupassant

When faced with an illegal question, you must choose your strategy carefully. The strategy you choose depends largely upon two factors: how you feel about the question and how much you want the job. Keep in mind, as always, that it never makes sense to answer a question if you are convinced that the employer plans to use your response to eliminate you.

1. You can answer the question and hope that the information won't be used against you.

2. You can answer the question and then explore how the employer plans to use the information.

3. You ask how the information relates to the job requirements (without answering the question).

4. You can refuse to answer the question because it is illegal.

82. Your Turn to Ask

One who asks a question is a fool for five minutes;
one who does not ask a question remains a fool forever.

Chinese proverb

The questions that you ask during an interview are as important as the questions that you answer because they enable you to

- ✔ assess whether you really want this specific job
- ✔ understand the employer's needs and goals
- ✔ build a working relationship grounded in two-way communication

1. What are the major responsibilities of this position?

2. Is there a job description? May I see it?

3. Why is this position open at this time?

4. How often has this position been available during the last five years?

5. What did you like most about the last person who held this job?

6. What would you like to see a new person do differently than the last person?

7. What qualifications do you look for in a candidate?

8. Why do you value those qualifications so much?

9. What are the greatest challenges and obstacles facing the person in this position?

10. How does this position fit into the organizational mission?

11. What are your goals and expectations for the person in this position?

12. What kind of resources and support are available for this position?

13. What do you see as the career path for someone in this position?

14. How would you describe the organizational culture?

15. Has there been much turnover in this department?

16. How would you describe the supervisor/manager's management style?

17. How many people would I be supervising? What are their backgrounds? How long have they been in their positions?

18. How will my performance be measured?

19. How much travel does this position require?

20. Does the company value creativity and risk-taking?

21. Has your organization dealt with a lot of change in recent years?

22. How does the organization tend to handle change?

23. Who does this position report to?

24. How much freedom would I have to set my own goals and deadlines?

25. What do people like most/least about working here?

26. Will I be able to meet the people that I would be working with before accepting the position?

27. Do you encourage professional development? In what ways?

28. Do you have an internal training program?

29. Is there a budget to attend professional conferences?

30. Is there anything else that I can tell you about myself?

31. What is the hiring process?

32. What is your timeframe for filling this position?

83. Closing Moves

Sell to their needs, not yours.

Earl G. Graves

When all of your questions have been asked (and hopefully answered), it's time to initiate your closing moves.

1. Start by expressing your appreciation for the opportunity to interview.

2. Restate your desire to work for the company.

3. If you're confident that there's mutual interest and you want to risk an aggressive closing move, review and summarize your best selling points and then follow up by asking the interviewer "Where do we go from here?"

4. Another (more aggressive) strategy is the assumptive close. In this scenario, you assume that the employer wants to hire you and try to close the deal by asking "When can I start?"

5. If you prefer a more subtle strategy but are confident that the employer is interested in potentially hiring you, you can volunteer your references as a potential next step or simply ask, "Where do we go from here?" Their response to this question will ultimately determine your next move.

Another aggressive closing strategy involves what salespeople call the "Ben Franklin close."

1. You start by asking the interviewer to share their perceptions of your suitability for the job.

2. Ask the interviewer's permission to look at that information objectively. Then take out a blank sheet of paper, draw a line down the center, and mark one column Positives and the other one Liabilities.

3. At this point, simply record their observations without attempting to refute their beliefs.

4. When the list is complete, work on neutralizing their objections by restating your qualifications and providing new evidence in the form of stories and examples.

5. If you are convinced that the employer's objections are unfounded (but can't quite prove it) and you're in a position to propose a "trial purchase," you can offer to work on a temporary or contractual basis in order to prove you can do the job.

84. The Global Factor: Interviewing with Foreign Companies

The Law of Raspberry Jam: The wider any culture is spread, the thinner it gets.

Alvin Toffler

As businesses continue to globalize, the rules of cultural protocol become increasingly important, particularly in the context of non-Westernized companies and people. A few tips to help you master the basics:

1. Start by doing some cultural research on the customs and protocols of doing business with people from a specific country. However, you must use that information judiciously after determining how Westernized the interviewer is and the company's reasons for seeking an American manager/employee.

2. As long as you use the information wisely, country-based research should help you better manage the interview process and understand what to expect.

3. Though you should never try to change all of your natural mannerisms, you can make a conscious decision to adapt your body language and communication to the situation. If you know, for example, that direct eye contact is considered a sign of disrespect in Japan, you can make a conscious effort to control your body language.

4. Be more conservative in your attire, demeanor, and language. Don't use slang or idioms, call interviewers by their first name, or adopt any of the more informal practices that often characterize American business.

5. Don't prejudge. Set aside your biases and preconceptions in order to keep an open mind toward people and businesses that operate differently than you are used to. Rather than focusing on differences first, look for common ground.

6. Be sensitive to timing and show up as close to the scheduled interview time as possible. Although some cultures are notorious for their lateness, it's nearly impossible to know the interviewer's bias beforehand (unless you have a good networking contact), so err on the side of punctuality. It's better to show up on time and be asked

to wait than to show up after the scheduled time and discover that you're too late for the interview.

7. Keep your distance. Americans tend to operate (quite literally) at arm's length. Move over to the Middle East or Mediterranean countries and things warm up considerably. Instead of making any assumptions (and changing your distance a priori), take your cues from the interviewer.

8. Manage your expectations. Americans in general like to move quickly to close the deal, and interviewees usually like to move more quickly than interviewers. In many other countries, interviewers like to spend more time getting to know the candidate before they make any commitments. This can translate into lots of personal questions (which, in American companies, would definitely be considered off-limits). Remember that if you don't feel comfortable with the way they conduct the interview process, you probably won't feel comfortable working in their organization.

9. Don't trade ideologies. An interview is not the time to talk politics. Most interviewers aren't going to be interested in your views on terrorism or the politics of gender.

10. Be honest with yourself. As much as you want a job, it doesn't make sense to rush into something that isn't right for you. By taking the time to understand how a foreign company's culture may affect your career, you place yourself in a better position to make an informed choice.

11. Negotiating compensation with a foreign company has its own set of unique challenges. If there is an overseas transfer involved, you'll definitely want to know whether the company will pay relocation expenses as well as whether you'll get paid in American currency or in the currency of that country.

85. Salary Negotiations

A billion here, a billion there, and pretty soon you're talking about real money.

Everett Dirksen

Sooner or later the discussion between a candidate and an interested employer will turn to the subject of compensation. Many job hunters are anxious to know salary details early on in the process (in order not to waste time and emotion on companies who aren't willing to pay them enough). However, it is not in your best interest to introduce the subject into the process too soon.

1. Try not to talk compensation until you have a firm job offer. Until an employer decides that you are the best candidate for the job, you won't have maximum negotiating power.

2. Recognize that salary is usually a negotiable item. Most employers expect to negotiate beyond the first offer.

3. Be courteous. When it comes to talking money, let the employer go first because, when it comes to talking money, the one who mentions money first loses.

4. Whenever possible, negotiate directly with the hiring manager—in person. Human resources representatives and recruiters are not usually authorized to negotiate.

5. You won't get what you want if you can't ask for it. Employers who "steal" you may not respect you enough to pay you what you deserve. Bargains seldom command much respect after the purchase.

6. It is unusual for an offer to be withdrawn simply because you ask for more. Most of the time, the worst-case scenario is that they will stand firm and refuse to negotiate.

7. Know your own bottom line before entering into negotiations. If you aren't sure of your fair market value, go to Salary.com (www.salary.com) to learn more about the average salary at your level and in your industry.

8. Negotiate as a friend and equal who is seeking a solution that is equitable to both sides. For the negotiations to be successful, they need to be "win-win."

9. Negotiate base salary first plus commissions and bonus (if you are in a performance-based role). After that, negotiate benefits in descending order of importance.

10. Provide yourself with a cushion in anticipation of being cut back through counteroffers. Normally, you should feel comfortable asking for 15 to 20 percent more than the original offer or at least 10 percent over your bottom line.

11. If the offer is lower than you expected, make sure that you restate your interest in the position and desire to work for the company while expressing disappointment and concern (not anger) at the offer.

12. Never negotiate with pistols or deliver ultimatums. Instead, acknowledge your understanding that the hiring manager is operating under certain constraints and work with the manager to see how flexible he or she is willing to be.

13. Never trade today's guarantee for tomorrow's promises. You must meet today's needs from today's income.

14. Try to establish some wiggle room in the form of backup options. For example, "If you aren't able to offer me a higher salary, do you think that you could consider an extra week of vacation or a company car?"

15. When you agree on a package, get the offer in writing—even if you have to write it yourself and send it to the employer via registered mail.

16. Never accept an offer on the spot. Tell the employer that you are very interested in the position and would like some time to think about it. Ask them when they need your final answer.

17. Only you can determine whether an offer is sufficiently attractive for you to accept it. If you aren't completely comfortable with the terms, go back to the drawing board and see if you can work out the details with the employer.

86. Evaluating Job Offers

It's not hard to make decisions when you know what your values are.

Roy Disney

When you have a job offer, the moment of truth arrives. Do you want to take it? Here are some questions you need to ask yourself before making a final decision:

1. Did I meet the person who will manage me?

2. Do I think that I can get along with my new boss?

3. Have I met the people who I will work with?

4. Do I feel comfortable working with the other members of my team?

5. Where does this job fit in terms of organizational goals and values?

6. Do I understand the job responsibilities and expectations?

7. Do I think that I have the skills and experience to do the job right?

8. Where does this position lead in terms of career paths and direction?

9. Is this a dead-end job? Or is there room for growth and advancement?

10. Does the company treat its employees with respect?

11. Does the company have a lot of turnover?

12. Do I know why this position is available now?

13. Is the compensation acceptable?

14. Is the company competitive in its industry?

15. Does the company have a good reputation?

16. How often will I be evaluated? And on what basis?

17. Does the company provide any training?

18. Does this job enhance my skill set and career opportunities?

19. Do I feel good about this offer?

20. Would I prefer to keep looking for a better opportunity?

87. Say Goodbye to Your Job

Farewell, fair cruelty.

William Shakespeare

When you accept a new position, you may need to say goodbye to the job you still have. Regardless of how angry, upset, or annoyed you may feel with your soon-to-be-ex-employer, it's better not to burn any professional bridges on your way out the door.

1. First, determine how much notice you want to give. Two weeks has always been standard; however, if you are in a higher-level executive or professional position, it is courteous to give more (assuming you have more to give).

2. The first person at the office that you need to inform of your decision is your boss, because you don't want your boss to hear of your departure through the grapevine rather than directly from you.

3. Schedule a face-to-face meeting with your boss to inform him or her of your decision. Make sure that you present the information in a positive manner. Simply inform them of your decision to leave as well as your last day of employment. Express your appreciation for the opportunity to work with them.

4. Do your best to negotiate the terms of your leaving fairly. Review your projects to determine an orderly transfer of responsibilities.

5. Offer to train your replacement, if possible. If they haven't hired a replacement by the time you leave, consider making yourself available by telephone for the first few weeks after you leave.

6. After your resignation meeting with your boss, write your resignation letter. Address it to your boss and send a carbon copy to the human resources department. In that letter, make sure that you confirm your intention to leave and inform them of your last day of employment. Because this letter will become a part of your permanent record, *do not elaborate on your reasons*. Keep the note short and positive.

7. Schedule an exit meeting with the human resources department to discuss your benefits package. Review your insurance benefits and make a decision about when to terminate your health insurance coverage. You will be asked to make decisions about your 401(k) plan and other parts of your benefits package.

8. Terminations often cause hard feelings. Your goal, at all times, is to take your leave professionally and responsibly without burning any bridges behind you. One day you may need a reference or letter of recommendation from your former employer. You may even find yourself working with your former co-workers at some point in the future.

88. The Counteroffer

It ain't over till it's over.

Yogi Berra

Your mind has been made up and you're ready to go. But your current employer has other ideas and ups the ante with a counteroffer. Should you take it?

1. Review your reasons for leaving. Are you disappointed with the money, job responsibilities, opportunities for advancement, or something else? List your reasons below.

   _____

   _____

   _____

   _____

2. Review the terms of the counteroffer. Will it remedy your dissatisfaction or is it a short-term answer to a long-term problem?

3. What is your employer's intention? Do they genuinely want to meet your professional needs? Or is it an act of desperation because they can't afford to lose you right now?

4. If you elect to accept the counteroffer, how long do you plan to stay with your current employer? Will you continue to look around for other opportunities with other employers?

5. Picture yourself working with your current employer over the next year or two. How do you think that you will feel? Content? Frustrated? Angry? Bored? Record your feelings and reflect on them.

   _____

   _____

   _____

6. What is the history of your relationship with your current employer? Do you feel that they have treated you fairly? Do you believe that they will keep their promises to you? Are you concerned that they may retaliate against you for your perceived disloyalty to them?

7. If you are uncertain of the answers to any of these questions, talk to your boss and other people in the company again before you make your final decision.

Career Development Across the Life Span

Career development is an ongoing process. In this section, you will learn how to evaluate career opportunities and make successful and satisfying career decisions.

89. Career Planning: Taking the Time to Do It Right

Never put off till tomorrow what you can do the day after tomorrow.

Mark Twain

It continues to amaze me that most people spend so little time planning what kind of career and job they want compared to the number of weeks, months, and years they invest working in jobs and careers that they hate. No wonder there is so much unhappiness and dissatisfaction in the workplace. To make good choices, you need to understand what really makes a successful and satisfying career.

1. Money is important, but it's not the be-all and end-all of career success, and it's certainly not the only route to satisfaction. If you take a job strictly for the money without paying enough attention to what you will be doing to earn that money, you may be setting yourself up for frustration and unhappiness.

2. Good career planning involves marrying internal and external rewards. The key to a satisfying and ultimately successful career is to figure out the best way to earn money with work that uses your talents and is compatible with your personality style and values.

3. Career planning is not like vacation planning. Now that the dot-com bubble has burst, it's back to business as usual in the workplace. This means that most people aren't going to make enormous fortunes in a few short years and then retire to Greece to play beach volleyball and sail the Mediterranean.

4. Career planning is a continuous process in which you must constantly assess yourself, build your skills, expand your network, and connect with the job market. Don't wait until you need a job to start thinking about these crucial skills.

5. Seek out mentors. These are people who work in your field (or fields that interest you) who can support and guide your career development. Keep in mind that mentors are not parents or saviors; they are experienced and knowledgeable people who are willing to help you figure out—and go—where you want to go.

6. Expand your skills, experience, and network through professional, community, and volunteer activities. They will lend a new perspective to your current situation.

7. Consider lateral moves. The desire to advance through promotions and upward movement is both understandable and seductive, but there are times in your career when you may benefit from a lateral or sideways move in order to gain more experience and expand your skills before moving upward.

8. Memorize and practice the term "job enrichment." This means looking for opportunities to take on new projects and responsibilities in your current job to demonstrate that you are a team player and learn valuable career and organizational skills.

9. Balance your desire to stand out with your need to fit in. Successful careerists are often good team players as well as individual performers.

90. What Do You Want to Be Now That You're Grown Up?

How old do you have to be before you feel like a grown-up in your own head?

Bob Greene

This is a question that some people, regardless of age, never seem to stop asking. If you find yourself repeating this phrase long after you're an adult, this is what you need to know to answer that question for yourself.

1. You have to make your own career choices and decisions. People who choose careers in order to please parents, teachers, or other people in their lives often feel like impostors—as if they're living someone else's career dream (which, of course, they are).

2. An adult career choice is an emotionally authentic choice. It is based on personal talents, values, personality style, and needs and usually involves the ability to balance financial needs and goals with intrinsic motivations.

3. Career choices often involve compromises. But you are the one who dictates what those compromises will be. If you can't live with a certain compromise, don't make it—no matter what other people may tell you that you should do.

4. There's nothing unrealistic about having a dream. As George Bernard Shaw once said, "You see things; and you say, 'Why?' But I dream things that never were; and I say, 'Why not?'"

5. There is no one perfect job. Every job has its weaknesses and liabilities. The key is to find the best job for you at any given point in your life. To do that, you must learn the art and skill of both career planning and job hunting.

6. Keep experimenting. Most of us learn from experience. Sometimes you have to try new things to figure out whether they are right for you. Never be so afraid to make a mistake that you are unwilling to try. The key is to learn from your mistakes—not avoid them altogether.

91. Is a Career Change Right for You?

We cannot live the afternoon of life according to the program of life's morning.

Carl Jung

There's no reason to expect that the career that you chose at 20 or 30 or even 40 will automatically be right for you at 50 or 60. If any of the following circumstances apply to you, you may want to consider a career change:

1. You were passed over for a promotion and have been thinking that it might be time to explore new horizons.

2. Your last child just graduated from college, got married, or moved out of the house, leaving you with more time, fewer expenses, and greater freedom.

3. You have reached the top of your career ladder and are hungry for new challenges and opportunities.

4. You recently celebrated a milestone birthday and have begun to think about your career goals differently.

5. You have a new baby in your family and your priorities have shifted.

6. You recently experienced a tragedy that has given you pause to reevaluate your needs, values, and priorities.

7. Your interests have changed.

8. You are having a midlife crisis.

9. Your industry or profession has undergone a dramatic transformation and is no longer right for you.

10. You are feeling the need to take more risks.

11. You need more security and stability.

12. You are encountering age discrimination in your field and realize that it is time to redirect your energies into an area where there is more opportunity for you.

92. Taking a Professional Survey

To hunger for use and to go unused is the worst hunger of all.
Lyndon B. Johnson

You may not know enough about your career options to make an informed career decision at this point in your life. To remedy that problem, you'll need to do some job market research:

1. Start by making a general list of your personal and professional interests. In the beginning, you want to include everything that you think of, regardless of how remote that option may be. Later on you can winnow that list down to the choices that you deem "do-able."

2. Write down your top interest and think about it carefully. What is it about that subject or activity or environment that fascinates you so much?

3. Explore your interests more deeply by researching

   - companies or organizations that produce related products or services
   - schools that teach related skills
   - job possibilities that are connected to your interests
   - people who are involved with the same interests

4. Create an action plan for yourself that includes process goals that will enable you to learn more about the fields or professions related to your interests. Your plan might include talking to people who work in the field, taking a class, or volunteering your services.

5. Listen to your heart. Are you excited about the possibility of pursuing a career that is more closely related to your interest? If your answer is a more cautious "maybe," continue your research and exploration so that you can make an informed decision.

6. If you discover that your top interest doesn't translate into viable career options, move on to the next item on your list and repeat the process until you uncover a promising direction.

7. If you are still undecided after completing several rounds of this exploratory process, you probably need to think more creatively about ways to combine your interests, skills, and financial needs.

93. Going Back to School (At Any Age)

Our best chance for happiness is education.

Mark VanDorn

In the process of deciding on a new career direction, you must also figure out exactly what kind of training, education, and credentials you will need to accomplish your career change goals.

✔ Contact the professional associations in the field or talk to people who are already working in this area to determine what qualifications and education they consider most valuable.

✔ Investigate the educational programs that are available to you, including

- traditional degree programs at community colleges, colleges, and universities

- individual courses at academic institutions taken either as a non-degree student or for credit

- online degrees and courses specifically related to your new career field

- professional development programs and workshops offered through professional associations or academic institutions

✔ After you have determined your educational needs and options, you may need to figure out how you are going to pay for them. Some potential options: loans, grants, scholarships, tuition reimbursement benefits, home equity loans.

✔ Family considerations are also important. During a career transition, you may need to enlist the financial and emotional support of your family.

✔ Your previous educational experience can also become a factor in your success or failure. If there is something in your past that can potentially prevent you from becoming a good student in the future, now is the time to deal with it. If you need professional assistance from a therapist or guidance counselor, reach out for the help you need.

94. Planning Your Career Change Strategy

Life is what happens to you while you're busy making other plans.

John Lennon

When you have decided on your new career choice, you will need to develop and implement a career change strategy. To do so, you must be able to ask—and answer—the following questions:

1. Do you need to go back to school for additional education or training?

2. If you need additional training, have you researched the programs that are currently available to you?

3. Is your current employer willing to finance your education?

4. If not, how do you plan to finance it?

5. Have you applied for grants, loans, or scholarships?

6. Would you consider a job change primarily to obtain tuition reimbursement that will advance your career objective?

7. If you can enter the new field without additional training, have you identified the names of specific jobs for which you can apply?

8. Have you identified your transferable skills in order to facilitate a lateral move?

9. Have you rewritten your resume in the best format for career changers?

10. Have you created a networking strategy that you can use to help you with the career change process?

11. Do you know the names and locations of the professional associations and the services and programs that are available to career changers?

12. Have you contacted the associations and programs for assistance and information?

13. Do you know and subscribe to the industry trade journals?

14. Do you read and respond to classified ads in trade publications?

15. Have you considered writing and publishing your own classified ad?

16. Have you considered—and identified—apprenticeships, internships, temporary jobs, or volunteer activities that will add to your experience and skill base?

17. Have you talked to your alumni placement office?

18. How much time do you realistically think it will take to make this transition?

19. Have you established viable goals that will keep your career transition on track?

20. Have you created a one-year plan?

21. Have you created a two-year plan?

22. Have you created a three-year plan?

95. Job Search Strategies for Career Changers

When you come to a roadblock, take a detour.

Mary Kay Ash

Making a career transition without losing income or going back to school on a full-time basis often requires resourcefulness and creativity.

1. Use a functional or combination resume that describes your skills and qualifications while de-emphasizing your chronological work history.

2. Conduct informational or exploratory interviews to reality-test your career decision and build a targeted and supportive network of contacts.

3. Use networking as your primary job search strategy. Ask family, friends, and acquaintances to introduce you to people who work in the new field or industry (or who know people who work in your target area).

4. Get involved in the professional associations where the people in your new career industry or profession congregate, learn, and support each other's professional development.

5. Don't waste too much time on recruiters or headhunters. For the most part, these professionals do not work with career changers.

6. Obtain a referral to a quality career counselor who is familiar with your area of interest and can coach you through the career transition process.

96. The Self-Employment Option

My son is now an entrepreneur.
That's what you're called when you don't have a job.

Ted Turner

Many people dream of being their own boss. Are you cut out for the rigors of self-employment? This checklist will help you determine whether you have what it takes to succeed on your own terms.

1. I am very ambitious.

2. I can deal with rejection.

3. I am self-motivated.

4. I like to work long hours.

5. I like to do things my own way.

6. I have strong opinions about how things should be done.

7. I trust my own judgment.

8. I am a self-starter.

9. I enjoy working alone.

10. I have good communication skills.

11. I am comfortable with risk.

12. I am more of a leader than a follower.

13. My family and friends are supportive of me.

14. I enjoy being creative.

15. I am very independent.

97. Building Greater Security

If security no longer comes from being employed,
it must come from being employable.

Rosabeth Moss Kanter

We live in turbulent economic times that require resourceful and creative strategies to build greater financial and emotional security. The following checklist, which is adapted from my book *How To Be Happy At Work*, contains some ideas to get you started:

1. Do good work. Although this may not guarantee a spot on your current employer's payroll, it has several other advantages:

   - It will make you feel better about yourself if you have to re-enter the job market.

   - It will improve your marketable skills.

   - It will motivate others to help you.

   - There is no substitute for a good reputation.

2. Practice *kaizen*. This is a Japanese term for a continuous learning mentality. Work hard to grow your skills and expand your expertise.

3. Be a team player. Although the term "team player" has obviously become a cliché in today's workplace, it still carries meaning when it refers to the process of collaboration and the ability to work well with others.

4. Never get too comfortable. For people who like the work life orderly and predictable, the current workplace climate is a real challenge. Without becoming paranoid, keep in mind that nothing lasts forever and approach each work day with as much energy, commitment, and enthusiasm as you can muster.

5. Develop a spirit of creativity and innovation. With so much emphasis on gaining the competitive edge, organizations increasingly value the work of people who are always on the lookout for new and better ways to help the organization maintain its competitive edge.

6. Know how to job hunt. Job searching, as I hope that I've demonstrated in these pages, is a skill set that can be learned and refined. One form of security is knowing that you can find another job when you need it.

7. Feed your Rolodex. Although the actual Rolodex may be going the way of the dinosaur, the concept of expanding your network of contacts is alive and well. Rather than rest on your social laurels, take the initiative to meet new people both within and outside of your current organization.

8. Develop supplemental revenue streams through 401(k) plans, prudent investments, side businesses, and lucrative hobbies. Then, if something does happen to your job, you will still have income.

9. Know yourself—what you like, what you're good at, what you need in order to be successful. Then direct your energies toward the kinds of activities and environments that are most energizing and comfortable for you.

98. Evaluating Your Job Security

Life is a daring adventure or nothing at all.

Helen Keller

1. On a scale of 1 to 10 (with 1 being the least secure), how secure is your current job?

2. Is your job more or less secure than it was one year ago? Two years ago? Five years ago?

3. Looking realistically at the future, do you think that you will still have the same job next year? Two years from now? Five years from now?

4. If your job security is diminishing, what can you do in the immediate future to feel more secure?

5. Do you have an investment strategy? If not, do you need to consult with a financial planner or consultant?

6. Do you have marketable skills?

7. Is there anything that you can do to increase your marketability?

8. Are you worried about age discrimination?

9. If you are worried about age discrimination, how do you plan to deal with it productively?

10. Do you know how to conduct an effective job search?

11. Is your resume outdated?

12. How active is your network?

13. How can you begin to expand your network of contacts now (before you need it)?

14. Is self-employment an option for you?

15. What do you see as the obstacles to self-employment?

16. Do you consider yourself employable? If not, what do you plan to do about it?

17. Are you being too passive about your future?

99. Quitting Your Job Cold Turkey

Leave them while you're looking good.

Anita Loos

Before you conclude that your only choice is to stay in a job that isn't right for you, examine some of the assumptions that may be leading you toward that particular conclusion.

1. I should be grateful that I have a job and not look a gift horse in the mouth.

   A job is not a gift. It is a contract in which you exchange your professional services for compensation. If you aren't happy with that arrangement, you have every right to look for something that suits you better.

2. The devil you know is better than the one you don't know.

   Yes, it could be worse somewhere else. But it could also be better. Are you convinced that the job you have really is the very best job you can get?

3. I'll never make as much money anywhere else.

   If you're convinced that you're being paid more than fair market value for your services, your job is undoubtedly in jeopardy anyway, because it's only a matter of time before your current employer arrives at the same conclusion.

4. Maybe things will get better.

   Sometimes things do improve—and sometimes they don't. What evidence do you have that your workplace is moving toward becoming a better place to work?

5. It would be disloyal for me to look around.

   In case you haven't heard the news, loyalty is dead. Should people at your company decide that they no longer need your services, will they be as faithful to you?

100. The Downside of Downsizing

If you can't laugh about it, then you are doomed.

Tom Peters

Whenever an employer makes the difficult decision to downsize or reorganize, the impact reverberates throughout the organization. Before you breathe that proverbial sigh of relief that you still have your job, steel yourself for the reality of your work life for the foreseeable future.

1. Feelings of insecurity are a common byproduct among survivors during and after a reorganization. Having a job today is no guarantee for the future. To feel better about the job you have, start planning your own exit strategy.

2. Poor planning and poor communication abound. In a workplace that is likely to be characterized by secrecy, mistrust, and power struggles, employees thirst for direct communication and more information. Don't be afraid to ask for what you want and need to do your job well. If you don't take the initiative, no one else will do it for you.

3. Power struggles are commonplace as the remaining employees vie for resources, authority, and power in the newly restructured organization. Figuring out how to build alliances with people under this new regime is an important career/job responsibility.

4. Burnout is bound to set in when you are expected to do the work of more than one person with the same (or even fewer) resources. Regardless of how unrealistic your employer's expectations may be, try to maintain your own sense of balance and locus of control.

5. After a downsizing, it's common to see divisive relationships and feel a lack of management credibility and commitment because no one knows who to trust, especially with regard to bosses and management. Use your people skills to restore trust and communication among your colleagues and co-workers as well as the person you report to.

101. Your Career Progress Report

I know the price of success: dedication, hard work, and an unremitting devotion to the things you want to see happen.

Frank Lloyd Wright

You need to set goals and monitor your progress (or lack thereof) in order to build a successful career. The following worksheet is designed to help you keep track of that information. You can create similar worksheets for goals in other areas of your life, such as promotions, networking, education, finances, and so on.

JOB SEARCH GOALS

Goals: _____

_____

Plan: _____

_____

Year 1 (Indicate progress): _____

_____

Year 2 (Revise plan): _____

_____

Year 3 (Revise plan): _____

_____

Index

Q–R

S

T

U–Z